vanity fair

vanity fair

PHOTOGRAPHS OF AN AGE

1914-1936

Introduction by

JOHN RUSSELL

Edited by

DIANA EDKINS RICHARDSON

Designed by

MIKI DENHOF

Clarkson N. Potter, Inc./Publishers

DISTRIBUTED BY CROWN PUBLISHERS, INC. NEW YORK

Many of the illustrations contained in this
book initially appeared in separate issues of *Vanity Fair*
from 1914 through 1936. These illustrations
are protected by individual copyrights, all of which have been
renewed by The Condé Nast Publications Inc.

Published by Clarkson N. Potter, Inc.,
One Park Avenue, New York, New York 10016
and simultaneously in
Canada by General Publishing Company Limited

Vanity Fair is a registered trademark of The Condé Nast Publications Inc.
Manufactured in the United States of America
Compositor: Dix Type Inc.
Printer: Rapoport

Library of Congress Cataloging in Publication Data
Main entry under title:
Vanity fair: photographs of an age, 1914–1936.
Includes index.
1. Photography—Portraits. I. Edkins Richardson, Diana.
TR681.F3V36 1982 779'.2 82-7682
ISBN: 0-517-546256 AACR2

10 9 8 7 6 5 4 3 2 1

First Edition

CONTENTS

ACKNOWLEDGMENTS

Special thanks go to Carol Southern, William P. Rayner, and Paul H. Bonner, Jr.,
whose patience, cooperation, and support throughout the project was invaluable.
I wish to also thank the following people for their assistance
in the preparation of this book: Cynthia Cathcart of the Condé Nast Library, New York,
for her tenacious assistance in every facet of the project;
Tracy Jones and Lillian Stanley for their thorough compiling of the research;
Sally Brown for typing with ease and humor under great pressure;
Richard Cole for his technical advice. Several individuals have been extremely valuable
in tracking down particular photographs and information.
They are Julian Bach; Amy J. Browne; Bonnie Ford and Barbara Puomo Galasso of the
International Museum of Photography at George Eastman House, Rochester, New York;
Frances McLaughlin Gill; Anne Horton, Sotheby Parke Bernet; Susan Kismaric, associate curator,
the Department of Photography at The Museum of Modern Art, New York;
Toby Quitslund; Juliet Man Ray; Joanna T. Steichen; Richard Tooke, supervisor of
Rights and Reproductions, The Museum of Modern Art, New York. D.E.R.

We gratefully acknowledge permission to reprint from the following museums and libraries:
Pages 2–3, 7, 13.
Courtesy of the Library of Congress, Prints and Photographs Division.
Pages 4, 5, 27, 59, 123, 124, 140, 185.
Collection of the International Museum of Photography at George Eastman House,
Rochester, New York.
Reprinted with the permission of Joanna T. Steichen.
Pages 77, 83, 121.
Collection of The Museum of Modern Art, New York.
Gift of the photographer.
Reprinted with the permission of Joanna T. Steichen.
Page 74.
Collection of The Museum of Modern Art. Gift of James Thrall Soby.

FOREWORD

During the winter of 1977 as I was organizing the Condé Nast archives, I came across two locked file cabinets. No one knew where the keys were, but my curiosity led me to have the locks broken. When I opened the drawers I felt I was looking into a time capsule; hundreds of photographs, clearly old, most in excellent condition, were neatly stuffed in the cabinets. As I began to go through them, I realized they were from *Vanity Fair;* the majority, in fact, had been commissioned by the magazine. By the time I finished I had a vivid sense of the particular circumstances in which *Vanity Fair* flourished. An era of history, both social and photographic, lay before me. *Vanity Fair* brought to a wide public a sense of portraiture, which set a style used thereafter both commercially and artistically. In many cases the subjects of these portraits were photographed at the very inception of their careers, long before their images became fixed in the public mind, giving them a unique freshness and immediacy. In other cases, the photographs are essentially the very ones that have fixed the images, the ones that have lingered ever since on the edges of our memories. In this book we have selected the best of these remarkable photographs.

DIANA EDKINS RICHARDSON
Curator of Photographs
The Condé Nast Publications Inc.

Frank Crowninshield
Unpublished, no date
Lusha Nelson

INTRODUCTION BY JOHN RUSSELL

The period of *Vanity Fair* magazine was one in which great work was done almost as a matter of course in portrait photography. An imaginative editor who wanted a photograph of someone of consequence could count on getting it not from an all-purpose journeyman but from a photographer of genius: Man Ray, Berenice Abbott, Edward Steichen, August Sander. In no other field of effort open to an editor was the level of achievement so consistently high. It would not have been possible before, and it would not be possible today, for an editor to have his pick, almost without question and for what now seems an almost laughable fee, of work that will live as long as people want to look at photographs. This was an age of almost delirious opportunity where portrait photography was concerned, and it may well be Frank Crowninshield's greatest achievement as editor of *Vanity Fair* that he made the most of it. Hardly ever did he print a pedestrian portrait photograph. Image after image, throughout the history of the magazine, now strikes us as a classic of our century.

Such is the quality of these portraits that the photographer seems in retrospect to have had very much the upper hand in *Vanity Fair*. Not only was it difficult for any writer to compete with him, but even where his work was reproduced quite small, as it often was, and possibly cropped, it went its own way in its own space. It dictated the terms on which it would be seen. It was on the basis of a direct and complete contact that the reader got to know what Joseph Conrad looked like, and Albert Einstein, and Arnold Schoenberg, and Bertrand Russell. These were unforgettable images; it was a happy day when novelist, physicist, composer, and philosopher stalked the amiable pages of *Vanity Fair,* along with deposed royalty, dog breeders, tennis champions, and the more presentable politicians. Sometimes the captions were inane; high marks cannot be accorded to the editor who nominated Marcel Proust for the Hall of Fame "because he brought Paul Morand before the public." But what mattered was that the photographs in *Vanity Fair* added up in the end to an honor roll of twentieth-century men and women.

Quite possibly it helped that the photographers in question so rarely got star billing. As a physical object, the photograph needs a protective darkness in which to ripen, and something of the same sort could be said of the great photographers who contributed portraits to *Vanity Fair*. Nobody talked them up at the time. Man Ray never thought of himself as first and foremost a photographer. Berenice Abbott was in Paris at a time when eminent people were pleased and surprised if anyone wanted to photograph them. There was no market in the age of *Vanity Fair* for the portrait photograph as a work of art. Neither galleries nor collectors nor museums showed any interest in it. Even in *Vanity Fair* itself, prestige attached rather to "art photographs"—naked children on the beach, or painstaking remakes of classical still lifes—than to the portraits from which we would now hate to be separated. This may or may not have been galling to the photographer, but it certainly made for ideal working conditions. Privacy, discretion, unstressed commitment—these were some of the things that made this the heyday of portrait photography, just as they had favored the achievements of Eugène Atget. Photography of this kind in the 1920s and early '30s had no glamor. It made very little money. But whereas the more obviously ambitious photographs of that time now often look both dated and arty, these portraits are a landmark in the history of human exchange. Men and women of genius were scrutinized by their peers, disinterestedly, and Frank Crowninshield had the wit to know it.

It is time that these portraits were set free to live a life of their own. They belong to the history of photography, and to the history of humankind, more than they belong to bound volumes of *Vanity Fair*. But without *Vanity Fair* they would not have added a specific something to the awareness of thousands of people at the time when they were first available. So the history of *Vanity Fair* is worth examining too, both for its role as a center of hospitality for great photographs and for the magazine's own more general evolution.

In no sense, of course, was *Vanity Fair* regarded by its contemporaries as a photography magazine. It was a magazine to *read* as much as to look at. What endeared it to a discerning public, in that context, was that it aimed to combine the characteristics of both the little and the big magazine. This is a distinction not often insisted upon now that shifts in taste are giving both the little and the big magazine a bad time, but before World War II it meant a great deal. There were people who lived for little magazines, never tired of talking about them, and died a small death when the mailmen brought them a day late. And there were people who never opened a little magazine but had a lifelong dependency on big ones. Given *Life* magazine, they were twice themselves. Given *Hound and Horn* or *The Dial,* let alone *La Nouvelle Revue Française* or *Der Sturm,* they looked out the window.

Intercourse between these two groups of people lacked energy, direction, and point. Romance was ruled out, and friendship made precarious, if one person fainted dead away at the sight of Ezra Pound's emendations of T. S. Eliot while the other was more interested in the height of the First Lady's hemline.

It would be easy to take the path of disdain in this matter. Little magazines were and still are about difficult books, difficult art, and difficult music. Big magazines tend to be about fashion, investment, the rich, interior decoration, cosmetics, show business, gourmet food and drink, "dream vacations," high heels, and low calories. Big magazines are ephemeral by

Percy Grainger
August 1917
Maurice Goldberg

their very nature, whereas it is the ambition of the little magazine to print the article, story, or poem that will last a hundred years.

But it is also true that many little magazines are tedious beyond redemption, whereas big magazines—above all, those that flourished before the heyday of television—may offer as telling a commentary on their times as many an academic history. There are little magazines as

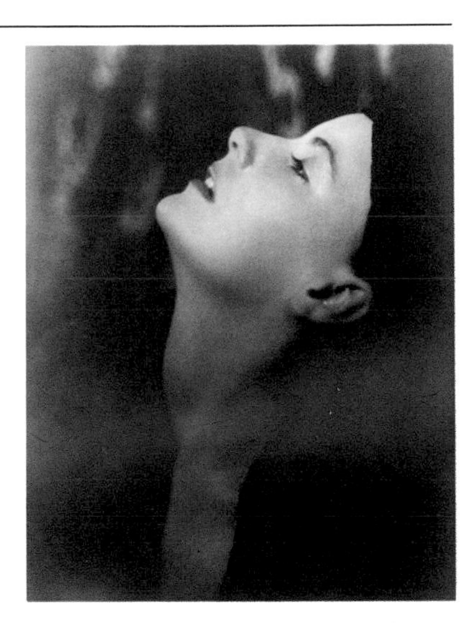

Greta Garbo
September 1926
Arnold Genthe

ridiculous as anything in Gogol, and there are big magazines that sweep us along by the forlorn grandeur of their ambitions and the misplaced confidence of their analyses. The big magazine is a repository of all that was hoped for, dreamed about, and taken for granted at a particular moment in time. Not to respond to a bound set of *L'Illustration* or the *Illustrated London News* is to miss out on a direct line to the past, and one that is worth any number of bad poems and misbegotten short stories. People who look down on fashion, sport, and food as subjects for serious study should look up Stéphane Mallarmé on the uses of the bloomer for the woman bicyclist, William Hazlitt on the fight between Bill Neate and the Gas-man, and Colette, *passim,* on the *cuisine bourgeoise* of Burgundy.

The nineteenth century knew this. What might be called the mixed-economy magazine came naturally to societies in which the magazine—big or little—operated as preacher, teacher, jester, and general counselor. In Paris the *Revue Blanche*—arguably the finest of all little magazines—was primarily a review of literature, art, and music, and as such counted virtually every great name of the day among its contributors. But it also touched on politics, economics, international affairs, divorce reform, industrial relations, and (a first, this, for any little magazine) the Swiss armed forces.

Before radio, and before television, magazines had a flexibility and a freedom of attack that arose from the fact that they had virtually no competition when it came to handling serious problems in a nationwide way. Newspapers are dead by dinnertime, no matter how much those who write for them would like to think otherwise, whereas magazines hang around. In New York the *Delineator* began in 1873 as a women's fashion magazine, but when it enlarged its character from 1894 onward and campaigned for women's suffrage, divorce reform, and the improvement of living conditions for women in homes and public institutions, its double identity turned out to be of international interest and validity.

Equally relevant is the case of *The Smart Set,* which began in 1890 as a magazine written by and for members of New York society and evolved into a magazine of much wider interest, whose first purpose—in the words of its editor in 1913—was to "provide lively entertainment for minds that are not primitive." That editor,

Jean Cocteau
March 1922, Paris
Delphi

Willard Huntington Wright, did not stay with the magazine long, but since he was the first American editor to print contributions by James Joyce, Gabriele D'Annunzio, D. H. Lawrence, and Ford Madox Ford, he may be said to have lived up to his ambition.

Common to all these adventures was the dream of a first-rate big magazine that would have a first-rate little magazine pouched somewhere inside it. Such a publication would serve the big-magazine public as a broad shoulder or rounded breast on which to recover from the stresses of the day, and for the little-magazine public it would revive one of the basic meanings of the word "magazine": a store of high explosive.

Vanity Fair, as it was owned by Condé Nast and edited by Frank Crowninshield from 1914 to 1936, had a double identity that endeared it to many thousands of readers. It had it from the start, moreover. Modeled expressly on "the great English pictorial weeklies," it had its full share of the silliness for which those weeklies were often conspicuous. In the month of November 1914, for instance, when it was clear that World War I was going to last much longer and be infinitely more destructive than had initially been thought, *Vanity Fair* kept right on going with "The Poodle as Companion" and the implications of the return of the stiff shirt cuff for men. If it got around at all to the war, it was to say that the Kaiser and his home circle were bearing up very well in difficult times. As for the general direction of the war, readers were assured that the Grand Duke Nicholas of Russia was "the ablest general alive" and just the man to pull his country through. But then, *Vanity Fair* was to the end a monarchical magazine.

Woodrow Wilson
April 1921
Arnold Genthe

In this, as in everything else, Frank Crowninshield knew perfectly well what he was doing. Editing *Vanity Fair* was the art of the possible, as far as he was concerned. "We do not attempt," he said in May 1914, "to rectify our industrial evils or to correct our crying civic abuses." *Vanity Fair,* in his view, was addressed to "people of means, who cultivate good taste, read good books, buy the best pictures, appreciate good opera, love good music and build distinguished houses." Crowninshield believed that in no other country had the number of such people increased with such rapidity. "Everywhere we go, East and West," he said, "we meet with people of discrimination and good taste, sophisticated in many directions, clever, and full of a wide and varied culture. These are the people for whom we hope to edit our magazine."

What he had in mind, in other words, was the surreptitious reeducation of a bunch of people who needed advice but were too pleased with themselves to invite it. In order to do this, he went along with what really sold the magazine. It was a deal, and a fair one.

He knew that it was important to put his readers in a good humor. People will stand for almost anything if you can make them laugh. Few men have ever been as funny as P. G. Wodehouse, and it is an indication of Frank Crowninshield's flair as an editor that during Wodehouse's first years in America he printed him as often as P.G.W. could come up with the copy. (He even printed him under the pseudonym of Pelham Grenville, his two given names, to skirt monotony in the magazine's table of contents.) Robert Benchley was another early contributor. Humor does not always wear well, but there is no doubt that a great many people bought *Vanity Fair* for the jokes, both verbal and visual, and that Noel Coward was only one of the very funny people whom it published at a time when they could very well do with the check.

Like every other editor, Frank Crowninshield was at his best and most committed with aspects of life that touched him personally. Music bored him, for instance, and although musicians, both male and female, were often seen and spoken of in the magazine, music itself was rarely discussed in a serious way. But the theater! Ah, the theater! *That,* he loved. *There,* there was no compromise. Corsets and corsetieres might sell the magazine in its first months, but *Vanity Fair* came straight out in September

1914 with a long obituary of the Duke of Saxe-Meiningen and an estimate of his achievement as a Shakespearean stage director. The theater, its editor said, "is the modern world's greatest amusement and diversion," and there is no sign that he ever wavered in this opinion.

He was also way ahead of most other editors, whether of newspapers or of magazines, in his feeling for modern art. Modern art in the first years of *Vanity Fair* had a certain outrageous interest for some of its readers, but it was not big business, it was not easy to see, and it had no institutional support. Nor was there much to read about it. People who cared about it were pretty much on their own, and *Vanity Fair* could have left them there without losing a single subscriber.

Georges Auric
Unpublished, no date, Paris
Photographer unidentified

It did nothing of the kind. New art was discussed in *Vanity Fair* in exactly the same terms as new everything else, and as something that every intelligent person would naturally want to know about. This was Frank Crowninshield's own wish, beyond a doubt, but some of the credit should go to one of the magazine's regular critics, Frederick James Gregg, who did not only the legwork but most of the explaining.

It was in January 1915 that *Vanity Fair* floated an idea that did not find general acceptance for another thirty and more years: that New York was "the world's new art center." Not long before, *Vanity Fair* had printed some "Cubist Poems" by the American painter Max Weber. ("A magical word, Cubism, these days," it said.) Nor could any general-interest magazine have done better, sooner, about some of the great names of twentieth-century art. Already in January 1915, for instance, there was a long article on Henri Matisse, with Edward Steichen's now-famous portrait of Matisse to go with it. In March 1915 there was what must have been one of the earliest color reproductions in this country of a painting by Picasso; and in June 1915 Frederick James Gregg wrote that "for us, the most important art of all is that of our own time." These were the terms in which Frank Crowninshield set about the education of his readers, and they were nothing to be ashamed of.

The readers of *Vanity Fair* in its first years were not taxed beyond their probable endurance. But they were led, almost without knowing it, to think that there was something about Henri Bergson, the philosopher; about Maxim Gorky, the novelist and playwright; and about W. B. Yeats, the champion of poetic drama, that might make it worth their while to know them better. With dancers like Nijinsky, Pavlova, and Duncan, they needed no persuading. The word "choreographer" took some time to make its way into *Vanity Fair,* but Frank Crowninshield knew that this was the era of the great individual performer in dance. It was the individual that people wanted to see, and to read about, just as the actors and actresses who got their names into *Vanity Fair* were people who could carry a play of their own accord. Crowninshield knew that there was a quality about such people that no amount of press

James Joyce
Unpublished, no date, Paris
Berenice Abbott

agentry or skillful public relations could counterfeit. The plays in which they appeared might not last well, and their names may have long been forgotten, but there was something about George Arliss and Gladys Cooper, and even about Irene Castle, that people did not forget. Like Robert Henri the painter, and Percy Grainger the composer, they had fulfilled faces.

It was characteristic of Frank Crowninshield that he got everything about Hollywood just right. *Vanity Fair* began at a time when the movies were still something of an exotic novelty for its readers, and it ended with the talking picture well launched and Hollywood just entering upon its period of greatest ascendancy. The magazine kept on the right course, all the way. Not only did it present a choice of movie actors and actresses that stood the test of time, but it even made the transition from the moving to the still picture without loss of quality.

This was not as easy as it sounds. The period in question was one in which the image of the actor and actress on the screen was almost as remote from everyday life as is the image of the actor and actress in the Kabuki theater, Makeup, lighting, mandatory expression—all seem to us today to have dated almost beyond belief. And those traits were carried over unchanged into the portrait photographs that were handed out by the studios. Those portraits come from somewhere in the prehistory of truth in photography, and we find it impossible to take them seriously. If there is a real human being somewhere at large within them, he or she has been stylized out of sight. It was the achievement of *Vanity Fair* that from time to time—not always—it beat the system and presented film stars as "real people." And it was as real people that they took their place in the honor roll that is the subject of this book.

We can look at *Vanity Fair* in many ways: as social history, popular history, the history of taste, and in a small way the history of political convictions. But the magazine was at its very best when it came to the look of people. It has many other claims to our attention. It printed short contributions—many of which would have been unacceptable to any other large-public magazine—by Gertrude Stein, T. S. Eliot, Bertrand Russell, Aldous Huxley, e. e. cummings, and Edmund Wilson. (Virginia Woolf refused, though she was tempted by the fee.) It put the case for the new in art, music, and literature, whether in passing or by implication. But it was in portrait photography that Frank Crowninshield really showed his hand, then and later.

He had the touch of gold, in that matter. By the end of World War I he had published portraits by Alvin Langdon Coburn, Edward Steichen, Gertrude Käsebier, Alfred Stieglitz, and Baron de Meyer. *Camera Work* itself could not have done better. Even those readers for whom one photograph was much like another must have been impressed subliminally by the fact that again and again and again what faced them on the page was a definitive likeness, a likeness never to be bettered, a work of art in its own right. Rodin, the man-mountain; Picabia, the practised rascal; Matisse, the obsessed workman; Nijinsky, the nonpareil of the dance—all were caught once and for all in *Vanity Fair,* along with people to whom no one now gives a second glance.

"Frankly frivolous" were the words used of *Vanity Fair* in some of its inaugural publicity. Frank Crowninshield was not in the editor's chair at that time, and when he did take over the magazine a year later he was careful to give a more balanced account of his intentions. *Vanity Fair* under his direction had, as I have said, a double identity. But much of it was still frivolous, whether "frankly" or not, and we can sense that toward the end of World War I he had trouble achieving an ideal balance in the table of contents. He was at his best, and *Vanity Fair* was at its best, after the war came to an end.

What this meant in practical terms was that the magazine could range the world with an impartial curiosity. Frank Crowninshield was an American, he loved America, and he was always delighted to discover a new talent or summon an old one. He was also a New Yorker, and if he thought that, for instance, August Belmont had done a lot of good for the New York public, he was happy to have Belmont in the magazine. He liked Americans to be large, difficult, and demanding, like Eugene O'Neill, Theodore Dreiser, and H. L. Mencken, but he was no less attentive to the ephemeridae who spawned on Broadway and in Hollywood. In fact, he lived America, ate and drank America, and even bathed in America.

Paul Claudel
February 1929,
Washington, D.C.
Edward Steichen

But the climate of the 1920s made it possible for him to range far and freely in other countries as well. He knew that there were people in Europe who should be talked about in *Vanity Fair:* James Joyce, Igor Stravinsky, Erik Satie, Paul Claudel. He knew that in England there was something called Bloomsbury, and he was forty if not fifty years ahead of most New Yorkers in his understanding of it. He knew that Bertrand Russell, Aldous Huxley, and G. K. Chesterton were among the most provocative English writers of the day. He knew that the Moscow Art Theater had a director, in Stanislavsky, and an actor, in Kachalov, who would be discussed as long as theater existed. He knew that there was a group of younger composers in France called "Les Six," and that the novels, stories, and poems of D. H. Lawrence were going to give people a great deal to think about.

The thing to do, therefore, was to get these people into *Vanity Fair* without frightening its readers away. And a classic instance of how to do it turned up in the issue for March 1922, in which James Joyce, the author of *Ulysses,* was interviewed by Djuna Barnes, the author of *Nightwood.* There was no more question of *Vanity Fair* running an extract from *Ulysses* than there would have been of its running an extract from *Nightwood,* but the conjunction of Joyce and Barnes was something that not even *Hound and Horn* could have improved upon. As it happened, Djuna Barnes turned out to be a very good interviewer. She asked good questions, she got good answers, and she put them down plainly and without interruption.

She knew how to set the scene, too. By her own account, she was sitting outside the Café des Deux Magots in Paris when she saw someone who could only have been Joyce. This had to be the man of whom Ezra Pound had said that he was "the only man on the continent of Europe who continues to produce, in spite of poverty and sickness, working from eight to sixteen hours a day." Sitting at her table, he revealed himself as a man whose every word had to be quoted.

"All great talkers," he said softly, "have spoken in the language of Sterne, Swift, or the Restoration. Even Oscar Wilde. He studied the Restoration through a microscope in the morning and repeated it through a telescope in the evening."

"And in Ulysses?" *I asked.*

"They are all there, the great talkers," he answered. "They and the things they forgot. In Ulysses *I have recorded, simultaneously, what a man says, sees, thinks, and what such seeing, thinking, saying, does to what you Freudians call the subconscious. But as for psychoanalysis," he broke off, "it's neither more nor less than blackmail."*

Joyce was a snappy dresser, too. Djuna Barnes told her readers about

. . . the most delightful waistcoat it has ever been my fortune to see. Purple, with alternate doe and dog heads. The does, tiny scarlet tongues hanging out over blond lower lips, downed in a light wool, and the dogs no more ferocious or on the scent than any good animal who adheres to his master through the seven cycles of change.

He saw my admiration, and he smiled.

"Made by the hand of my grandmother for the first hunt of the season," he said.

That was the style of *Vanity Fair.* Never were its readers advised to read something that they might find too difficult. On the contrary: an editorial aside assured them that "it is a question in many minds whether Joyce, in *Ulysses,* has not pursued his theory too far for coherence and common understanding." But no one, however poodle-oriented and corset-constricted, could help inferring from Djuna Barnes's article that Joyce himself was a man of genuine fascination. And if Mina Loy's drawing of Joyce did not do him justice, they had only to wait until the magazine published one of the photographs of James Joyce by Berenice Abbott that gave us, in human terms, a definitive Joyce. Frank Crowninshield knew just how far he could push his readers.

He dealt in gossip, that is to say, but in gossip of high quality from the best possible source. After World War I was finally over, for instance, he must have heard that art, music, and literature were in full ebullition in Europe, and more especially in Paris. Other editors would have played safe and engaged a pliable hack—or, as is now the customary phrase, "a free-lance writer with a particular interest in the arts"—to cover these manifestations. Frank Crowninshield had a better idea. He went to Tristan Tzara, the pioneer Dadaist; to Jean Cocteau, the archetypal nimble-witted Parisian poet and novelist; to Erik Satie, the composer who had set Paris on its ear with his ballet *Parade* in 1917; and to Georges Auric, then in his early twenties, who looked at that time to be a very promising composer. He went to the people who made things, in other words, and not to the people who talked about things. Even in the little magazines, it was not every editor who did that.

Around that same time he published portraits of Picasso, Tzara, Satie, Gertrude Stein, Jacques Lipchitz, and Augustus John by Man Ray. He published portraits of D. H. Lawrence by Elliott & Fry, of Jean Cocteau and "Les Six" by Isabey, and of Claude Monet by Baron de Meyer. The archives of *Vanity Fair* also include portraits of Francis Poulenc by Man Ray, of George Grosz by E. Bieder in Berlin, and of Igor Stravinsky by a photographer whose name has got away. There are not agency photographs, whipped up in a hurry. They are lasting contributions to our knowledge of people who left their mark on our century, and they would never have been bought for, let alone appeared in, the "frankly frivolous" magazine that had been mooted in 1914.

As this is primarily a picture book, one or two quotations are in order. Tristan Tzara gave *Vanity Fair* for the issue of July 1922 what is still the best short firsthand account of the beginnings of Dadaism. "Dada," he began, "is a characteristic symptom of the disordered modern world." Readers then learned of the Dada manifestation of January 23, 1920, in Paris, in which Tzara, along with André Breton, Louis Aragon, Paul Eluard, Francis Picabia, and others had taken part. Some of the information was not of the kind to which they were accustomed—Tzara said, for instance, that "there are three hundred and ninety-one Presidents of the Dada movement. Anyone can become a President very easily"—and there is about Tzara's contribution to *Vanity Fair* a refusal to talk down that still shines out on the page.

As a surveyor of the Parisian scene in general, Tzara proved remarkably objective. He was as well able to take stock of the first performance of Stravinsky's *Mavra,* for instance, as he was to describe the dress worn on that occasion by Sonia Delaunay, one of the foremost painters of the day (and of our own day, since she lived to be nearly a hundred). And when it came to summing up his friends and colleagues, his six-line summaries are still valid.

Igor Stravinsky
November 1927, Paris
George Hoyningen-Huené

Here he is on Jean Arp, for instance. We know Arp as sculptor, painter, collagist, and poet, but here he is as Tzara knew him:

"Arp is Alsatian, but lives in Switzerland. He is an athlete, but then he is also a wit. One of the first apostles of cubism, he soon abandoned it to find a new method of expression: dadaism.

He was the first artist to employ new materials in order to produce the effect that other painters had until then achieved only with oils and canvas. His carpets, for instance, are brilliant and agreeable works of art.

Arp's drawings, reflections of ephemeral states of mind, spontaneous movements, as it were, of his hands, innocent of any preoccupations with esthetic laws, strike a new note in art. They teach us that the beautiful is a reflection and a result of endless vitality, that it should grow as freely, as will-lessly, as fingernails or hair: No one could decide whether an Arp drawing represents a woman, a siren, a piece of furniture or a cloud; his fantasy outleaps our visual habits.

And here is Tzara on Max Ernst, with whom he had spent a fateful summer in the Austrian Tyrol—the summer, we may now think, in which the European imagination took a decisive leap forward:

"Max Ernst is a well-built man, whose fine intelligence manifests itself even in his muscles, for he knows instinctively how to scale the most stern-faced summits and can support his body with three fingers. He is a Dadaist because his fancy refuses to be inclosed within the dogmatic prison of a school."

If these things, and others no less exceptional, had appeared in a little magazine published in Essen, Germany, or Nancy, France, they would have been anthologized long ago. Edmund Wilson, for one, was delighted to quote at length from Tristan Tzara's writing for *Vanity Fair* in his book *Axel's Castle* (1936).

No less extraordinary is "The Early Days of Pablo Picasso" by Max Jacob, which ran in *Vanity Fair* in May 1923. Max Jacob was one of the earliest and most discerning of Picasso's friends in Paris. He is known today for that friendship as much as for his poems and for his tragic death at the hands of Germans in 1944, but in 1923 he was nobody in particular. Nor had Picasso at that time a great American reputation. It took an inspired editor to commission this article, which is as remarkable for immediacy and deep feeling as it is for its evident authenticity. Jacob had known Picasso since he was "a fiery little boy of eighteen who made two pictures a day." He had called on him by invitation in the year 1899, to find "a band of impoverished Spaniards sitting on the floor in the fine studio, eating white beans." He knew at first hand that "Apollinaire, that great exponent of the new poetry, often worked only to please Picasso." "He seemed but a child," Jacob said of Picasso at that time. "His great black eyes, which have an expression so tense when he looks at one, so mocking when he speaks, so tender when he is moved, glowed with life under his low, wide, positive forehead. His hair was coarse, thick and smooth: today, one or two silver threads shine in its blackness."

It was with Picasso as it was with James Joyce. Frank Crowninshield did not tackle the work head on. If he reproduced one of his paintings, it was what we would now consider a safe and tame example. If Picasso was talked about in the magazine, it would be in terms of himself, as much as of his work. *Vanity Fair* was not in the business of aesthetics. It was in the business of getting people talked about. That was the spirit that animated, among much else, the interview between Glenway Wescott, novelist, and Arthur Lee, sculptor, in June 1925. This is by any standards a very amusing piece. The stories about Picasso, Matisse, and Brancusi ring true. The portrait of Gertrude Stein in Paris before 1914 rings true, likewise. "The real Beaux-Arts was Gertrude Stein's drawing-room, which we called the Sacred Wood. There was Gertrude Stein—her lucid eyes and her laughter—and her brother Leo with his laborious mind. There were Matisse, Derain, and Picasso. There were the rarest books and photographs, and if the guests grew interested in anything which required illustration, the Steins hunted, and brought them out, and turned pages, like a couple of librarians in Heaven."

There is no better short description of the Steins at home, any more than there is a better short description of Matisse's model, Bevilacqua, than the one that appears in the same article—"a model in the quarter who was the smallest giant in the world. He had great Assyrian calves, and a cavity in his chest the size of two fists." Where is the general-interest magazine today that regularly publishes pieces of that kind and quality? But then, *Vanity Fair* always had a hot line to Paris. In September 1917 it carried an account by Jean Cocteau of the ballet *Parade*. Today we all know that *Parade,* with its scenery and costumes by Picasso, its music by Erik Satie, its choreography by Léonide Massine, and its argument by Cocteau, was a landmark in the history of the stage—but that realization is of recent date, whereas *Vanity Fair* came out in a matter of weeks with what still stands today as a classic account.

It should by now be clear that in what might be called its foreign correspondence *Vanity Fair* had an exceptional sureness of touch. Frank Crowninshield took it for granted that his readers would be as interested in Sarah Bernhardt and Eleanora Duse as they were in the newest names on Broadway. If they weren't, he went ahead just the same. In this way the readers of *Vanity Fair* were told in plain words what great acting was like. This was done not in relation to any of the American players of the day, but in a European context. Arthur Johnson, for instance, said of Sarah Bernhardt in 1916 that "her voice, especially when employed on the noble lines of Racine, seems to be not a single musical instrument but an entire orchestra. Prose she uses as if she were playing on a rare old violin." And then there was the veteran English symbolist Arthur Symons, who said of Eleanora Duse in 1917: "When she is silent, her face has a mystery that is more significant than anything that she can say; when she speaks, her smile is like a smile, like a caress, like a person; her voice is itself a woman. It has its physiognomy, with mortal pallors, dim anxieties, strange tendernesses."

Gertrude Stein
Unpublished, 1934, Paris
Man Ray

Eleanora Duse
February 1924
Arnold Genthe

Vanity Fair did not do as well when it came to the English-speaking theater. It was not simply that the players were not of the same order. It was that the English-speaking public settled for less. To this day, big-scale, big-ambition acting is an embarrassment to many American playgoers. Faced with Irene Worth or Colleen Dewhurst at full stretch in a play of real stature, they don't know what to do with themselves. The great staples of Broadway during the lifetime of *Vanity Fair* were the musical and the undemanding comedy. As was the case with the music hall in England, these so nicely matched the temper of the times that there was never the distance, the element of strangeness, or the challenge to understanding that are presented by superfine acting in a foreign language—or, for that matter, by great English-language acting in a difficult masterpiece.

Perhaps for this reason, *Vanity Fair* did not excel in the area of day-to-day dramatic criticism. Dorothy Parker was not a negligible writer, but when she had to cover a group of recent plays that included *Smilin' Through* and Somerset Maugham's *Caesar's Wife,* she really did a very poor job. With the theater, as with other departments of life, *Vanity Fair* was at its best when the news came from a long way off. When it dealt with Broadway, the result could usually have come from a press release, with only minimal adjustment.

To have an idea of what was missing, we need only look at "Drawbacks of the Drama in

England" by P. G. Wodehouse, which ran in the magazine in December 1922. It was a funny piece, of the kind that Wodehouse turned out without apparent effort, but when the reader turned the page he had learned something serious about Broadway, and about the West End theater in London, in almost every paragraph. If we want to know why Broadway in 1922 seemed like paradise to some young writers, the answer is that it had "a platoon or covey of genuine, established, working managers, with definite offices where the young playwright can get at them when he wants them—men who make a habit of producing a certain number of plays each season and who consequently have to be supplied with those plays by someone."

And if we want to know something about London that is as true today as ever it was, Wodehouse has it ready for us. "The first requirement for a new theater," he says, "is an evil-smelling alley where you can put the stage door. In all the big cities of the world, managers prowl about the slums, and when they have found a dark cul-de-sac paved with old cans and bits of cabbage-stalk they leap ecstatically into the air and shout "My Gosh! What a spot for a stage door!"

It is never easy for a magazine editor to find writing of this order, with its concision of phrase, its sharpness of focus, and its freedom from cant. *Vanity Fair* had other contributions of this quality—Gilbert Seldes on W. C. Fields for one; the young Paul Gallico on Babe Ruth, for another; and Bobby Jones ("Robert T. Jones, Jr.") on golf, for a third—but there were also many occasions on which the name was right but the substance was not. It is not given to every writer to be at his best for a specific magazine; and if the essay, the undemanding short story, and the teasing in public of one old friend by another have now gone out of style, *Vanity Fair* must bear some of the blame. Something in this is owed to the passage of time. Every generation has its accepted set of references, its mandatory tone of voice, and in particular its own idea of what is amusing. Posterity will not read our contemporaries as we read them. It will notice, as we sometimes do not, when the fingers have done the writing and the mind was somewhere else. There was a lot of finger work in *Vanity Fair*. Some of it was by great local names of the day, like George Jean Nathan and Dorothy Parker. Some of it was by eminent Europeans—Englishmen who almost died of languor before they got to their last sentence, Frenchmen and Frenchwomen who did not survive translation, Italians and Hungarians who should never have got off the boat.

Babe Ruth
January 1935
Nickolas Muray

This was not a matter of ill will or failing intentions. There are very good writers who simply cannot write short. There are subjects that simply cannot be tackled in two pages. There are key names of the moment that evaporate in print. And there is the matter of the environment. Like every other mixed-purpose magazine, *Vanity Fair* had to take into account the preoccupations of some very silly people. Contributors had to reckon with a circumambient fatuity that not all of them were able to beat back. They were not themselves in such conditions, any more than the Olympic champion swimmer is himself when he endorses toothpaste. Those are the hazards of the mixed-purpose magazine, and it is nobody's fault if the name of D. H. Lawrence in the table of contents of *Vanity Fair* raises hopes that his little squib does not fulfil.

In this respect, as in others, *Vanity Fair* took a turn for the worse at the end of the 1920s. Every magazine has its natural span of life, and that span should not be exceeded. At fifty years' distance it seems inevitable that *Vanity Fair* should have foundered, as in fact it did, during the 1930s. In March 1914 it had—so the editor told his readers—"but two major articles in its editorial creed: first, to believe in the progress and promise of American life; second, to chronicle that progress cheerfully, truthfully, and entertainingly." It was difficult in the years of the Depression to believe in either the progress or the promise of American life in terms that would have been acceptable to the "sophisticated" people whom Frank Crowninshield had always wished to please. There are moments in human affairs at which "sophistication" implies anesthesia to right and wrong.

This is not simply a matter of taste. If people bought the magazine in 1934 for "picture features" like "Celebrities in Bed" and "When Kings Relax," there was a choice to which they were entitled. *Vanity Fair* was in business to sell dreams, and to give people hopes of a good time, just as much as it was in business to give them a glimpse of high culture. Frank Crowninshield himself made a lively defense of the role of magazine advertising in 1934. ("Romance, to women," he said, "is very often only another name for morale.") Nor did he altogether give up the attempt to bring reason and order to his readers' thoughts about public affairs. What he had done for Wilson, for Hoover, and for Coolidge he tried to do for Roosevelt in a piece by Walter Lippmann that ran not long after Roosevelt's election to the presidency. There is no reason to doubt that he was ever anything but a good and decent man who stayed with the agreeable side of things just as long as there was an agreeable side to find.

But the good pieces—the short story by the young William Saroyan, the long reportage of a classic French court case by Janet Flanner, and Gertrude Stein's easygoing, strictly-for-beginners backward glance at her years in Paris—became fewer and thinner. On politics, whether domestic or international, *Vanity Fair* began to express opinions that now seem too "sophisticated" by half: that the "sum total" of the first nine months of the Roosevelt administration had "many characteristics of a coup d'état," for instance. Hitler in December 1933 was encapsulated by *Vanity Fair* as "Handsome Adolf—A Law Unto Himself"; and eventually the magazine suggested that the only way out of America's problems was for the Constitution to be suspended (temporarily, of course) in the interests of an authoritarian government.

The time had come, decidedly, for *Vanity Fair* to shut down. And shut down it did, in 1936. It had lasted twenty-two years, under Frank Crowninshield's editorship, and on the whole he had carried out an almost schizophrenic policy with remarkable skill. But it is with magazines as it is with tyrannies: one day they seem everlasting and impregnable, the next day we wonder how they kept going so long. In its little-magazine aspect, *Vanity Fair* under Crowninshield lasted a very long time. Editing a little magazine is not something like banking or the law, in which you can reasonably hope to get better and wiser with experience. It is like mathematics or athletics—you burn out fast. Crowninshield did not burn out fast—above all, perhaps, in his relation to portrait photography. In that matter, he set a new standard for the big-public periodical press, and one that has never been equaled, let alone excelled. What he wanted was not "brilliant" photography. Still less was it "outrageous" photography. He wanted dense, weighty, truthful photography. To the extent that he got it, more often than not, the photographs in this book are genuinely and most memorably the portrait of an age.

JOHN RUSSELL
New York 1982

the teens

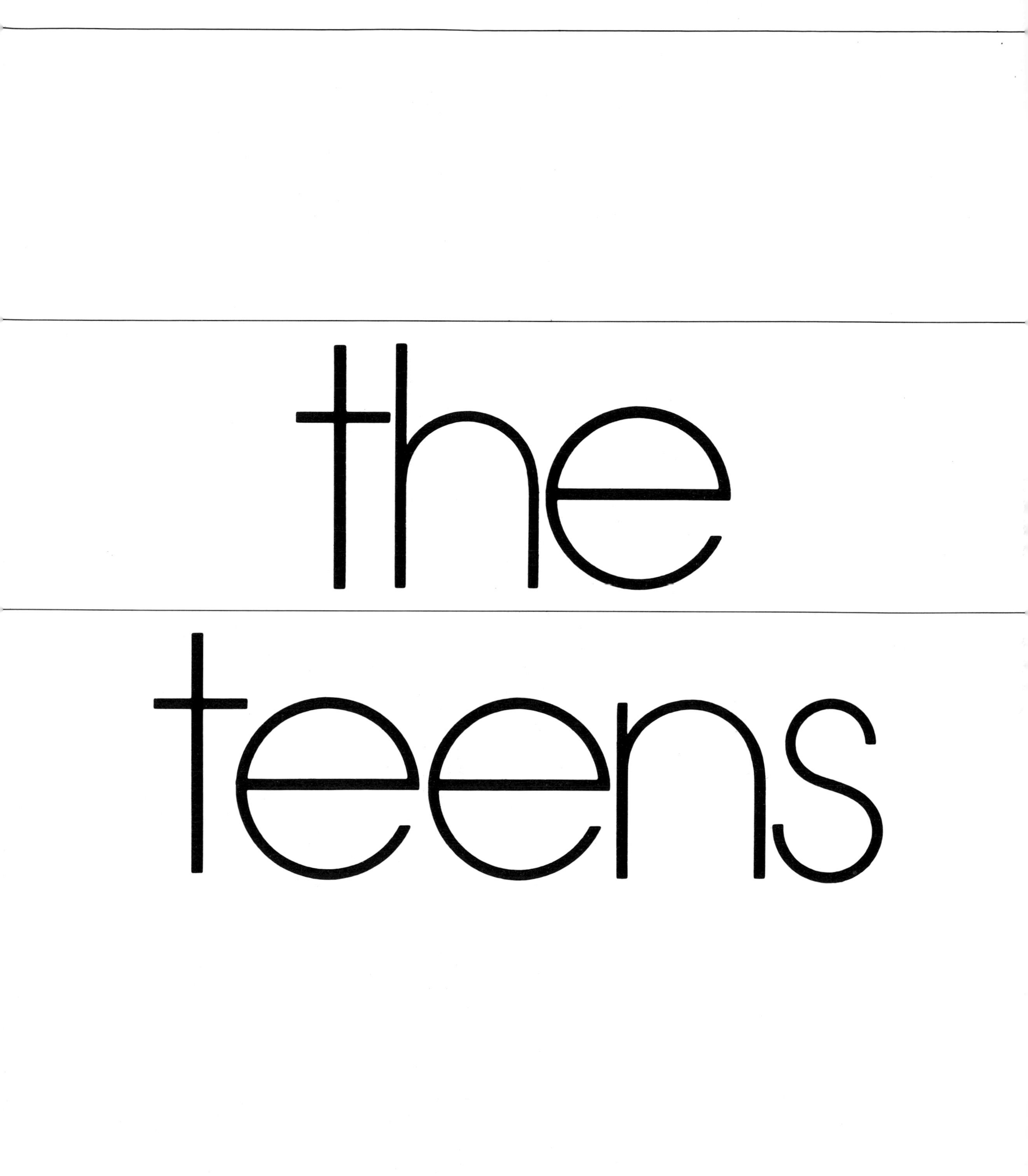

John D. Rockefeller
March 1919
Arnold Genthe
In 1923 John D. Rockefeller, age seventy-nine, was described in a caricature piece, "See the Conquering Heroes," as "A man of sufficient private means to employ two golf caddies—one to carry his bag and one to beseech him, by all that is oily, to keep his head down."

Henri Matisse
January 1915
Edward Steichen
There was more quarreling about Matisse, shown here at work in Paris, than about any other painter of the epoch. His *Nude with the Blue Leg,* shown at the International Exhibition of 1913, had "surprised New York, disgusted Chicago, and horrified Boston."

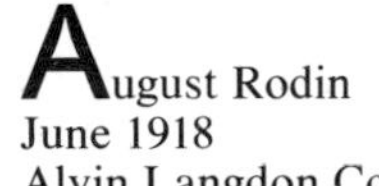

August Rodin
June 1918
Alvin Langdon Coburn
This portrait was taken at Meudon, Rodin's home, shortly before his death. Stephen Haweis wrote describing Rodin's bedroom, "upon a little table, stood a volume of Richer's *Human Anatomy,* and a candle—light reading —if he happened to waken in the night! I believe it was almost the only book he ever read."

Maxim Gorky (Aleksei Maksimovich Peshkov)
June 1914
Alice Boughton
In 1906, at the height of his fame, Gorky had come to the United States hoping to arouse sympathy for the revolutionary movement in Russia, but was bitterly disillusioned by his unsympathetic reception. Back in Russia at the time of this photograph, he was being tried on charges of blasphemy stemming from his novel *Mother,* written in the United States.

William Butler Yeats
October 1915
Arnold Genthe

THE COMING OF WISDOM WITH TIME

Though leaves are many, the root is one.
Through all the lying days of my youth,
I swayed my leaves and flowers in the sun;
Now I may wither into the truth.

W. B. Yeats

Francis Picabia
November 1915, New York
Alfred Stieglitz
Picabia, a French painter of Cuban ancestry, was an influential leader of the avant-garde in Paris. During his 1915 visit to New York he declared that "upon coming to America it flashed on me that the genius of the modern world is in machinery and that through machinery art ought to find a most vivid expression."

Otto Dix
Unpublished, 1907, Cologne
August Sander
Dix fought in World War I and returned to Düsseldorf haunted by the horrors he had witnessed. As a disciple of German Expressionism he depicted the sordid world of prostitutes and swindlers with a painful precision and intensity.

Anna Pavlova
December 1915
Eugene Hutchinson
In 1898, at the age of seventeen, Pavlova made her debut as a *première sujet* at the Imperial Opera House; in 1909 she danced with Nijinsky; and in 1910 she made her American debut. She wrote, "I remember that I used to practise some steps or poses—frequently for an hour at a time. I have known young girls to stand near a hand-rail at the side of a wall, and carry one leg through the first three movements of the Rond de Jambe for more than half an hour."

Vaslav Nijinsky
May 1916
Baron de Meyer
In 1907 Nijinsky made his debut and became principal dancer of Diaghilev's Ballet Russe. *V.F.* said of him in 1914, two years before he became the director of the Ballet Russe, ". . . of all modern male dancers Nijinsky is certainly the most famous. Although but twenty-six years old, the young Russian-Pole has already captivated most of the civilized countries of the globe."

Geraldine Farrar
February 1915
Baron de Meyer
She made her singing debut in America at the Metropolitan Opera House at age twenty-four. Said *V.F.* of her Carmen, ". . . That such an essentially Latin role should have been so well portrayed by an American is a matter for deep gratification."

Maxine Elliott
July 1917
Arnold Genthe
Star of both stage and screen. She had just finished her new film, *Fighting Odds*. "Has just left our shores in order to engage in relief work in England."

Maurice Prendergast
November 1915
Gertrude Käsebier
Pictured here at fifty-six, "He is one of the most joyous of painters. . . . He is one of the men who is introducing imagination into American decorative art."

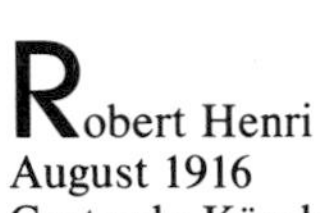

Robert Henri
August 1916
Gertrude Käsebier
The American society painter responsible for leading the New York realists in a revolt against academicism with his exhibition "The Eight." Their movement would soon become known as the "Ash Can School." In 1916 *V. F.* wrote, "While the famous Armory Show of 1913 was going on, he showed his attitude on this subject by a single remark. He said: 'I am sorry that this exhibition could not be continued forever.' "

Sir Arthur Conan Doyle
March 1920
E. O. Hoppé
The author and creator of Sherlock Holmes, sixty-one years old in 1920, was described with the comment that "the life, philosophy and writings of Sir Arthur Conan Doyle have been completely altered in their courses, as the result of many investigations which he has recently made in spiritualistic phenomena."

H. G. Wells
June 1919
E. O. Hoppé
"His real merit as a prophet is not so much his evocation of the world in 1960, as an incomparably clear vision of the world in 1923," Philip Guedalla wrote of Wells. "One thinks of him as a pair of bright eyes, watching the world alertly, and not without malice."

Helen Keller
September 1919
George Grantham Bain
Helen Keller, who had "demonstrated better than anyone else that speech is possible without recourse to the spoken word," was about to appear in a "photoplay" based upon her life.

Henri Bergson
May 1917
Campbell Studio
The French philosopher who made philosophy a fashionable indoor sport in America was in New York to talk about France and the War. Ten years later Bergson would win the Nobel Prize for Literature.

Ignace Jan Paderewski
September 1918
Arnold Genthe
"The world's foremost pianist, a great statesman and orator, Ignace Jan Paderewski takes a natural place among the super-men of the world."

George M. Cohan
March 1914, New York
Moffett Studio
"Cohan," said *V.F.* in 1922, "has risen in critical estimation from a soft-shoe artist and patrioteer to a playwright who, in plays like *Broadway Jones* and *Get-Rich-Quick-Wallingford,* has shown us the beginnings of a genre, American comedy."

Olive Terry
January 1916, London
Ellis and Walery
The Terrys were one of the most distinguished of English theatrical families. In 1916 there were nine members bearing the family name playing on the London stage. Olive, a timeless beauty, was the daughter of the famed actor William Morris and Florence Terry.

Elsie Ferguson
November 1917
Arnold Genthe
Among stage stars wooed by the movies was Elsie Ferguson, shown here on the eve of the release of her first film, *Barbary Sheep*. Describing the numerous skills she'd acquired in the movies, she included "the intricate details of murdering gentlemen, whether by poisoning, strangling, shooting or stabbing."

Lionel Barrymore
December 1918
Colotta
The much admired character actor was on an extended American tour in Augustus Thomas's play *The Copperhead*. "He has consistently given his public acting that *is* acting: barks, grunts, growls and snorts; and his eyebrows rise and fall faster than an Empire State elevator," said *V.F.* in 1932.

George Arliss
August 1918, New York
Baron de Meyer
At fifty, George Arliss was about to begin a tour of the American West in his characterization of Alexander Hamilton. "Mr. Arliss, though an Englishman by birth, has long been identified with the American stage, where he has stood head, shoulders and monocle above a legion of Anglo-American actors as an interpreter of beguiling scoundrels, wily diplomats and unscrupulous gentlemen of all ages and nationalities."/Page 24.

Elsie Janis
Unpublished, no date, London
Malcolm Arbuthnot
"Famous mimic, film-star, author and war veteran succeeds in the role of Impresario." In 1925 *V.F.* stated, "To all her old bag of tricks, she has added really striking imitations of Leonard Ulric, Beatrice Lillie and John Barrymore, in the last of which she executes the miracle of looking rather like Elsie Janis at one moment, and then, without any recourse to make-up, proceeding to look the very image of London's favorite Hamlet."/Page 25.

Irene Castle
September 1919, London
Malcolm Arbuthnot
Irene Castle, *V.F.*'s candidate for "the greatest ballroom dancer of them all," at twenty-six. "Her gestures have become fads, her mannerisms international vogues, and the history of her affectations is a history of fashion in the last decade and a half: bobbed hair, the Castle Hop, the debutante slouch, the boyish figure for women."

Eduard Steichen
January 1918
Self-portrait
Steichen at thirty-nine (still spelling his name Eduard); he had been at the vanguard of the twentieth-century controversy over, Is photography art? "Not satisfied with what he had done with the camera, he took to painting and made a success in that medium too." When he returned home after his service in World War I, he burned all of his paintings.

the
1920s

Grace George
April 1920
Baron de Meyer
Successful as both actress and producing manager, George was one of the most commanding figures of the theater at the time. She was starring in *The Ruined Lady,* the most brilliant comedy she had played since George Bernard Shaw's *Major Barbara.*

Billie Burke
October 1920
Alfred Cheney Johnston
In 1920, this popular actress, the wife of Florenz Ziegfeld, Jr., could be seen on screen in *Wanted—A Husband,* wherein "she is a struggling art student who spends five long, bitter reels searching vainly for a consort," and on stage in Maugham's *Caesar's Wife,* in which "she considers that she has one husband too many."

Lillian and Dorothy Gish
November 1921
James Abbé
"Appearing more than usually parentless in the Griffith production of *The Two Orphans*." The twin sisters had appeared together in a prior film, *Hearts of the World,* in 1918.

Lillian Gish
Unpublished, c. 1920
Baron de Meyer
The serious half of the Gish family (sister Dorothy was the comedienne), Lillian began her acting career at the age of five and was discovered on the Biograph lot by D. W. Griffith. She went on to become the quintessential helpless Griffith heroine in *The Birth of a Nation* (1915), *Broken Blossoms* (1919), and *Way Down East* (1920).

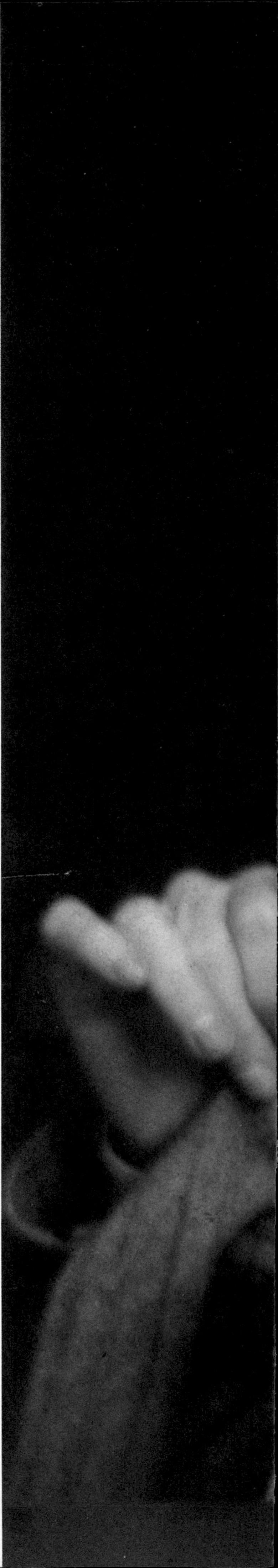

George Bernard Shaw
February 1920, London
Malcolm Arbuthnot
Shaw at sixty-four, five years before receiving the Nobel Prize for Literature. Critic A. B. Walkley wrote of Shaw, "he has succeeded by dint of writing *not* like other men and writing what other men do *not* like until he has made them like not only what he writes but even his way of writing it."

D. H. Lawrence
September 1921, London
Elliott & Fry, Limited
Lawrence, shown here one year after the publication of *Women in Love,* published a number of essays. In "Art and Morality" (1926) he wrote, "Let Cézanne's apples go rolling off the table forever. They live by their own laws, in their own *ambience,* and not by the law of the kodak—or of man. They are casually related to man. But to those apples, man is by no means the absolute."

G. K. Chesterton
October 1920, London
Speaight, Limited
The distinguished apologist for Christianity, pictured here at forty-six, was a frequent contributor to *V.F.* In one of a series of essays published in 1920, he said: "Once upon a time, men wrote their own epitaphs. What they wrote was generally doggerel; it was sometimes drivel; it was occasionally, in brighter intervals, blasphemy."

John Barrymore
January 1920, New York
Baron de Meyer (*left*)
August 1925, London
James Abbé (*right*)
In 1920, after his stage triumph in *The Jest,* Barrymore had just completed *Dr. Jekyll and Mr. Hyde* for the screen. St. John Ervine wrote: "In this man there is a unique power of expression that has not yet been fully revealed."
In 1922, Barrymore electrified the public with *Hamlet* at the Haymarket in London. We see him here backstage. Although the critics' praise was somewhat grudging, the audiences were unreservedly enthusiastic.

Six Obscure but Promising Young Actors
January 1921
Photographer unidentified
Top row from the left: Miss Mary Nash, the London society favorite; M. Georges Carpentier, connoisseur of vintage clarets and French pastry; Mlle. Alice Delysia, the Venus of the Rue de la Paix, specialist in repartee; Mr. Charles Chaplin, violinist, collector of Sung porcelains, imagist poet, and society favorite, who hopes some day to be featured on the screen. *Seated left:* Miss Joan Maclean, the English debutante, *right,* Mr. Knoblock, a Beau Brummell and playwright.

Charles Chaplin
January 1921
Baron de Meyer
Wrote e. e. cummings, "Homage—in the name of Beauty and Life—to the incomparable master of Make-Believe, the unparalleled Prince of Pretend: Charlie Chaplin, deity and doll, hero and clown, angel and penguin."

Claude Monet
March 1921
Baron de Meyer
At eighty, living at Giverny, Monet was the last survivor of the master Impressionists. Said *V.F.:* "He has suffered poverty, abuse and ridicule in the same proud and silent manner, as he today accepts the world's applause, fortune and fame."

Claude Debussy
Unpublished, no date
Photographer unidentified
Ernest Newman in 1928 noted: "In the last edition of *Grove's Dictionary* . . . Strauss is charged with the grave crime of being ultramodern, and we can all of us remember the time when Debussy was regarded as hyper-ultramodern."

Pablo Picasso
July 1922, Paris
Man Ray
The forty-one-year-old Picasso in a little-known casual portrait—almost a snapshot—by Man Ray. "He achieved world-wide fame and misunderstanding as the creator of Cubism," *V.F.* said of him in 1928; ". . . a few years ago he was an artistic anarchist, he is now named with Matisse as a dean of modernism."

Erik Satie
Unpublished, no date, Paris
Man Ray
In 1922 Georges Auric, one of "Les Six," wrote of Satie, whose aesthetic ideals had influenced the formation of the group: "Here at last was a real French musician. Stravinsky himself realized it by saying after a performance of *Parade:* 'There are three French musicians—Bizet, Chabrier and Satie.' "

Les Six
October 1921, Paris
Isabey
Five of "Les Six" are shown here photgraphed on the Eiffel Tower. The sixth member of this group, who appears in place of Louis Durey, is Jean Cocteau, the poet, who had assisted "Les Six" in arriving at the New Aesthetic. From left to right are Germaine Tailleferre, Francis Poulenc, Arthur Honneger, Darius Milhaud, Cocteau, and Georges Auric.

Tristan Tzara
June 1922, Paris
Man Ray
In "Some Memoirs of Dadaism," Tzara, one of the founders of the movement, described the Paris debut of Dadaism on January 23, 1920. "As for me," he wrote, "I read a newspaper article while an electric bell kept ringing so loudly that no one could hear what I said. This was very badly received by the public, who became exasperated and shouted: 'Enough! Enough!' "

Jean Cocteau
March 1922, Paris
Isabey
Cocteau operating one of the "phonographs" which explained the action of his latest ballet. He had invented this device for enormously magnifying the voice and imparting to it the characteristic nasal timbre of the phonograph. "Genius, in art, consists in knowing how far we may go too far," he wrote.

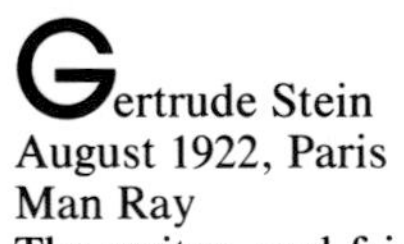

Gertrude Stein
August 1922, Paris
Man Ray
The writer, and friend and hostess to the "lost generation" (a Stein phrase), including Ernest Hemingway, F. Scott Fitzgerald, and Sherwood Anderson, shown here at her studio at 27 rue de Fleurus.

Ernest Hemingway
September 1928, Paris
Helen Breaker
Pictured here at age twenty-seven, two years after *The Sun Also Rises* was published. He lived in an austere carpenter's loft on the Left Bank.

F. Scott Fitzgerald
July 1925
Photographer unidentified
Fitzgerald, twenty-nine, upon the publication of *The Great Gatsby*. Charles Shaw noted: "He believes true happiness to consist of the performances of all the natural functions, with one exception—that of growing old—while Sunday, Washington, D.C., cold weather, Bohemians, the managing type of American woman, avarice and dullness are his principal dislikes. . . . He is practically always on time."

Eugene O'Neill
Unpublished, no date
Nickolas Muray
"Not of the soil, O'Neill writes from inner sources but most eloquently of the humble or outcast. Our first cosmopolitan dramatist whose work has made Europe suspect we may have a national soul after all."

A Group of Russian Masters
June 1923, New York
Arnold Genthe
In one room in New York, five of Russia's great men. On the left, Moskvin, a leading character actor, next to Konstantin Stanislavsky, teacher, actor, and theatrical producer. Seated, Feodor Ivanovich Chaliapin, considered the greatest operatic figure in his time; Katchaloff, leading Russian tragic actor; and Savely Sorin, artist, whose *Portrait of Anna Pavlova* hangs in the background./Pages 54–55.

Jacques Lipchitz
December 1922, Paris
Man Ray
The Polish sculptor at thirty-one, in his studio in Montparnasse. "How many times," said Jean Cocteau, "have I seen Lipchitz made ill when an indiscreet visitor has been looking for a likeness in one of his statues—irregular buildings inhabited from top to bottom by a soul."

George Grosz
Unpublished, no date, Berlin
E. Bieder
"Since Forain, there has been in the art of Europe no more bitter or ironic spirit," said *V.F.* of Grosz in 1933. "But the ever-recurring note of cruelty in his cartoons is only a weapon with which he combats political wrongs and social evils."

E. Bieber
Berlin

Isadora Duncan
June 1923
Edward Steichen
Duncan in the Parthenon, in her characteristic costume—an adaptation of the Greek tunic, complemented by several colored scarves draped from her shoulders. Rodin had said of her art, "The brilliance of her spirit makes the glory of the Parthenon live again."

Harald Kreutzberg
January 1928, Berlin
Baruch
Kreutzberg, solo dancer of the Berlin Opera house, was known abroad as the Austrian Nijinsky. He is seen here as the premier dancer in Max Reinhardt's production of *A Midsummer Night's Dream*. *V.F.* said, "Noted primarily for his grotesques, he has also made a reputation in the more conventional forms of pantomime."

Bronislava Nijinska
November 1922, Paris
Man Ray (*right*)
La Nijinska, here in the role of Kikimora in Larionov's ballet, was the sister of the world-famous Vaslav Nijinsky, a noted dancer in her own right, and chief choreographer with Diaghilev. Her ballets *Les Biches* and *Les Noches* are still frequently performed.

Léonide Massine
November 1923
Maurice Beck and Helen Macgregor (*left*)
The noted dancer and choreographer of the Ballet Russe, shown here in costume for *Le Carnaval*. Cocteau wrote about the production of *Parade*, in 1917, "Massine, who played the Chinaman, had a great ovation. . . . Among his minor accomplishments, he could produce an egg from his pigtail, spit fire and put out the eyes of missionaries. . . . his brilliant costume caused enthusiastic comment."

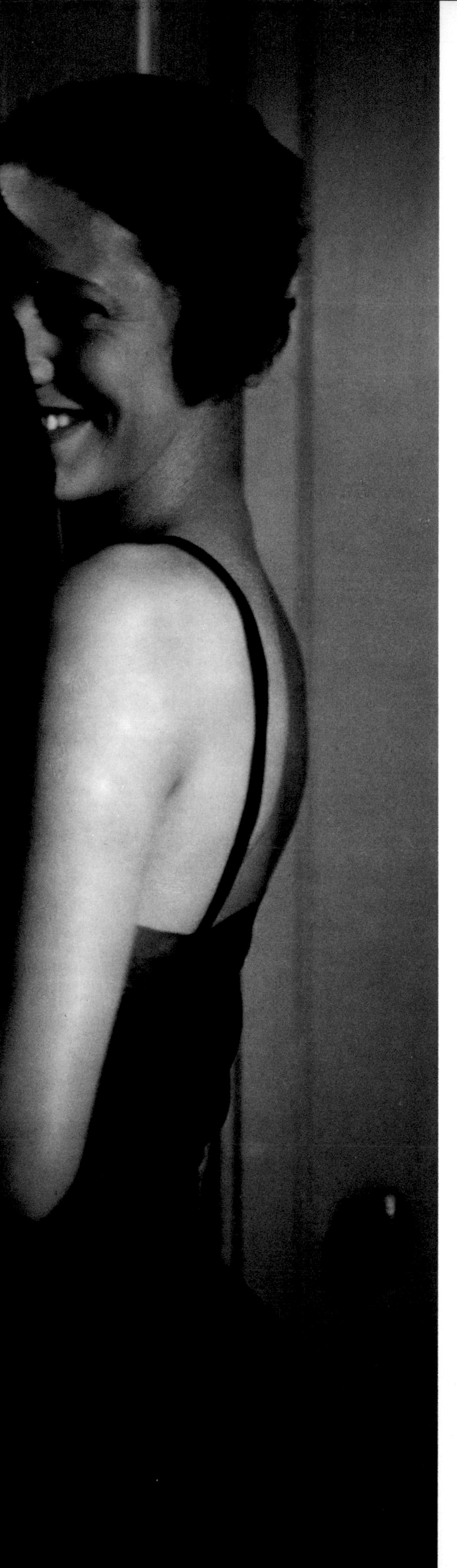

Gertrude Lawrence
April 1924
Edward Steichen (*left*)
September 1929
Edward Steichen (*right*)
The English actress as a Parisian Pierrot in André Charlot's London revue. In 1929 she deserted the musical stage to play in a comedy of manners, *By Candlelight,* by P. G. Wodehouse. Two years later she would star in Noel Coward's *Private Lives* in "the role of the bored young woman (opposite that of Mr. Coward as the bored young man)."

Douglas Fairbanks, Sr.,
and Mary Pickford
December 1922
Nickolas Muray
This celebrated couple were married from 1920 until 1935. Although they did not star in a film together until 1929, when they made *The Taming of the Shrew,* according to a rumor reported by Carl Van Vechten, Pickford "doubles for his leading woman, in costume, with her back to the camera, whenever the script calls for a love scene. It will be remembered that there are comparatively few love scenes in a Fairbanks screen drama."

Douglas Fairbanks, Jr.,
and Joan Crawford
October 1929, Santa Monica
Nickolas Muray
In a portrait of his wife, for the July 1930 issue of *V.F.,* Fairbanks wrote: "She is a ten-year-old girl who has put on her mother's dress—and has done it convincingly."/Pages 66–67.

Joseph Conrad
March 1924, London
Malcolm Arbuthnot
This photograph was taken shortly before Conrad's death. In an accompanying "Estimate of Joseph Conrad," the English critic and novelist Frank Swinnerton wrote that Conrad's books were "stolen from the heart of beauty itself, and were brooded over by a magician whose richness of understanding made him sometimes over-full of revelation. . . ."

Arnold Bennett
September 1927
Photographer unidentified
Bennett at sixty. In September 1914 the critic Henry Brinsley reviewing *The Price of Glory,* "an entirely new kind of who-stole-the-money story," compared Bennett's technique to "that of a Dutch school of painting—a use of detail so accurate, so lavish, so admirably marshalled that an effect is produced as of reality itself."

Aldous Leonard Huxley
May 1922
Photographer unidentified
Huxley, twenty-eight years old, after publication of *Crome Yellow*. In 1928 Huxley wrote in *V.F.*: "Across the modern world the shadow of that much-whiskered, library-haunting student, Karl Marx, lies dark and gigantic. Such examples could easily be multiplied. The retired and solitary writer can wield more than the power of a king or general without ever issuing from his lair, without ever making himself personally known."

Augustus Edwin John
May 1923
Man Ray
"His is the most beguiling figure in the Cafe Royal as well as the drawing-rooms of Mayfair," said *V.F.* of the half-gypsy Welsh portrait painter; "he is a rebel by racial inheritance, blending, in everything he does, the qualities of the ironist with those of the dreamer."

Will Rogers
March 1924
Edward Steichen
Alexander Woollcott wrote of Rogers: "In the village of New York, Rogers is the philosopher who sits . . . behind the stove at the post office and comments on the passing show for the enlightenment of his neighbors. Give him rope enough, and he'll hang all the humbugs in America."

Fannie Brice
June 1923
Edward Steichen
"The most finished artist of them all. . . . No one in America is so sure of her audience, so subtle in her burlesque, so much a mistress of expression, so skillful in turning the vulgar to artistic account." Brice starred in the *Ziegfeld Follies* from 1910 onward.

Sinclair Lewis
May 1925, Paris
Man Ray
Since the appearance of *Main Street* (1920) he had become one of the most popular novelists in America. By 1925, in spite of the rancor and dissension that his drastic satires had occasioned, *Main Street* had sold 750,000 copies and *Babbitt* (1922) 400,000. At the time of this photograph he had just been awarded the Pulitzer Prize for *Arrowsmith,* which he refused.

Willa Cather
Unpublished, October 1922
E. O. Hoppé
"No one else has so well expressed the new philosophy, the urge 'to live out our potentialities,' because no other novelist has so deeply felt the need of it, yet so vividly seen that such a philosophy should not mark a break with our past but an enrichment."

J. Pierpont Morgan
May 1924
Edward Steichen
Morgan's matchless library had just become the property of the public. This was the first publication of the portrait that Morgan had said he preferred above all other portraits of himself. In 1924 a single platinum enlargement of it was sold for a thousand dollars.

Josef Stalin (Joseph Djugashvilli)
Unpublished, no date
Acme Newspictures
Joseph Djugashvilli, proletarian, was raised to be a priest. He is shown here after delivering a seven-hour speech at a Congress of the Communist Party in Moscow. "Djugashvilli has taken many aliases," wrote *V.F.* in 1931, "but the last, the greatest, the enduring one is Stalin—'steel.' It fits him so well, that even Lenin on his death-bed cried, 'This man is too hard for me!' "

Bertrand Russell
June 1924
Florence Vandamm
Russell at fifty-two, while lecturing in America. In "Thoughts on Psychology and Politics," he concluded: "Psychology . . . does not teach us to despair of human nature; it merely enables us to see through the many shams and counterfeits which are offered in place of genuine kindliness, out of which alone all the best actions spring."

Albert Einstein
March 1923
Martin Höhlig

"The scientific world is now in suspense as to the outcome of the experiments which will verify or disprove this theory. It has already been established that the planet Mercury does not move according to the Newtonian laws, but in such a way as to corroborate Einstein's theory; and observations based on the eclipse of 1919 seemed further to justify it. The results of the calculations based on the eclipse of last September have not yet been made public, and the third cardinal experiment, is still in doubt; but if these conclusions bear out the others, the evidence in favor of Einstein's revolutionary hypothesis will have become overwhelmingly convincing."

Henry Ford
July 1926
Bain News Service
V.F. in 1922, "He has changed the whole rural life of America by lowering the price of motor cars; he has said 'history is bunk.' "

John Maynard Keynes
March 1928
Crafters
Baron Keynes of Tilton, monetary expert: "A year ago it was the failure of agriculture, mining and manufacture and transport to make normal profits, and the unemployment and waste of productive resources ensuing on this, which were the leading features of the economic situation. Today in many parts of the world, it is the serious embarrassment of the banks which is the cause of our gravest concern."

Clarence Darrow
September 1928
Nickolas Muray
Mencken on Darrow: "The marks of battle are all over his face. He has been through more wars than a whole regiment of Pershings. And most of them have been struggles to the death. Has he always won? Superficially, yes; actually, no."

Gloria Swanson
February 1925
Edward Steichen (*left*)
February 1928
Edward Steichen (*above*)
Gloria Swanson was one of the Mack Sennett Bathing Beauties. Cecil B. de Mille saw her during the making of a Sennett picture and offered her a contract. By the late 1920s she had long been the highest-paid woman in the world, and from 1920 until 1932 she produced her own films.

Adolphe Menjou
May 1927
Edward Steichen
"As an actor, Menjou dismisses murder with the lift of an eyebrow—marriage with a shrug of the shoulders, and passion with a twist of his well-clipped mustachio."

Claudette Colbert
March 1929 (variation)
Edward Steichen
"Emigrée, from France, ex-Art League student, in such earlier plays as *The Wild Westcotts* Miss Colbert had hidden her light—and her now famous legs," wrote *V.F.* in 1927. "But soon the theater world was aware of a new pair of rhapsodies of stocking silk."

Fred and Adele Astaire
July 1925 (variation)
Edward Steichen
In 1911, Adele Astaire and her brother Fred formed a successful Broadway vaudeville team. At the time of this photograph *V.F.* said: "Although Fred and Adele Astaire of *Lady, Be Good* have often been heard to swear that never, never NEVER could they be induced to dance at a night club, and though they could hardly be classified as a grasping boy and girl, the Club Trocadero finally lured them to its floor at a figure which caused Adele to swoon becomingly into her brother's arm."

Alfred Lunt and Lynn Fontanne
Unpublished, no date
Cecil Beaton (*left*)
August 1925
Edward Steichen (*below*)
These two gifted Theatre Guild players, married in 1922, were favorites of *V.F.*, appearing with great frequency. After a distinguished season in *The Guardsman,* a comedy by Ferenc Molnár, which inaugurated their partnership in the theater, the two players took part in a Shaw cycle produced by the Guild, playing in *Arms and the Man* and *Pygmalion* to full houses.

Katharine Cornell
December 1926
Edward Steichen
In 1921 Cornell married producer-director, Guthrie McClintic. Beginning with Michael Arlen's *The Green Hat,* in 1925, they had a highly successful theatrical partnership. She was among the first major American performers to form a repertory company.

Eva Le Gallienne
October 1927
Edward Steichen
Upon Le Gallienne's founding of the Civic Repertory Theatre in 1926, *V.F.* wrote: "She has betrayed of late a marked disposition to go it alone in the theater, without dependence on theatrical managers with their timorous notions about making money and all that sort of thing. Last season she wrestled with two of the more resisting plays in the Ibsen list and threw them both."

Helen Hayes
October 1927
Edward Steichen
Of this former child actress, *V.F.* wrote: "Helen Hayes, through her various flapper roles, has set a standard for this type in the theater. Now, she is slated to do the super-flapper, Shaw's Cleopatra."

Rudolph Valentino
June 1923
Maurice Goldberg
In October 1926, after Valentino's death at the age of thirty-one, Jim Tully wrote: "It would seem that nearly all screen people spring from the Salvation Army bread line. Valentino was no exception. He arrived penniless in America during the year 1913. Being an agriculturist, he dreamed at the time of a great farm in the West."

Pola Negri
June 1925
Edward Steichen
Pola Negri, the exotic Polish tragedienne, first came to the attention of the American public through her parts as royal mistresses and wayward gypsies under the wing of Ernst Lubitsch. When this photograph was published, she had just started filming *Half Roads of the World,* by Michael Arlen.

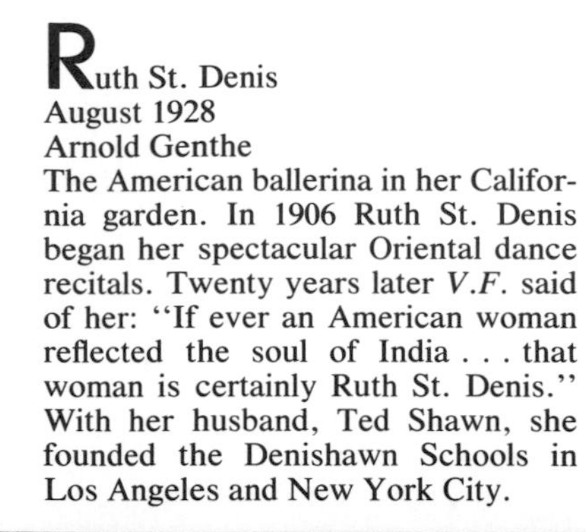

Ruth St. Denis
August 1928
Arnold Genthe
The American ballerina in her California garden. In 1906 Ruth St. Denis began her spectacular Oriental dance recitals. Twenty years later *V.F.* said of her: "If ever an American woman reflected the soul of India . . . that woman is certainly Ruth St. Denis." With her husband, Ted Shawn, she founded the Denishawn Schools in Los Angeles and New York City.

Agnes de Mille
June 1928, New York
Nickolas Muray
"She excels in character studies, in the deft juxtaposition of pathos and buffoonery. There is something of the plaintive clown about her and something of shrewd understanding. In a program which ranges from . . . a Degas dancer at rehearsal to a robust recapturing of the spirit of the gold rush of '49, she is an emotional actress, a ballerina and a comedienne."

Jascha Heifetz
February 1925
Nickolas Muray
The Russian-born violinist made his first public appearance at the age of five, and played the Mendelssohn Concerto when he was six. He came to America with his parents in 1917 at the age of fifteen, and made his debut in New York later that year. In 1925 *V.F.* called him "one of the most prodigious of living concert artists."

Vladimir Horowitz
June 1928
Photographer unidentified
The Russian pianist, following his triumphant American debut with the New York Philharmonic Orchestra. "St. Petersburg audiences crowded to hear him during the starvation days of 1922; both Europe and America have shown unprecedented enthusiasm over the nervous, tempestuous virtuosity of this twenty-five-year-old pianist."

Igor Stravinsky
Unpublished, no date
Photographer unidentified
"By the time the *Sacre* and Stravinsky reached America three years ago [in 1924], the enthusiasts had won out over the dissenters. And then Stravinsky with his habitual flair for the unexpected announced that Bach was the greatest modern of them all and that his slogan for the future would be 'Back to Bach!' "

Helen Menken
April 1925
Edward Steichen
January 1926
Edward Steichen
In May 1926 *V.F.* praised this actress for having undertaken "to play two women, neither of them a day under a hundred years old. She was the witch-like Ratwife in the mild, afternoon revival of *Little Eyolf* and she played the 399-year-old lady of *The Makropoulos Secret*. To be sure, the anguish involved was somewhat mitigated for Miss Menken by the circumstance that this last is a play about a singularly durable woman who had a potion that kept her looking not a day over thirty for centuries."

Conrad Veidt
October 1929
Edward Steichen
Conrad Veidt, considered the German equivalent to John Barrymore, had created his macabre portrayal in *The Cabinet of Dr. Caligari* and *Nosferatu*. "The pantomime of this German screen actor is one of the formidable arguments against talking pictures."

Sidney Howard and Clare Eames
October 1924
Edward Steichen
"Sidney Howard was a comparatively young man when he wrote *Swords,* his first play. After that time, he devoted most of his time to forms of writing other than drama. Perhaps, it was his marriage to Clare Eames which brought him back to his first love."

Maurice Chevalier and
Yvonne Vallée
August 1928, Paris
George Hoyningen-Huené
Chevalier—whose career covered nearly two decades—was about to make his American debut in vaudeville and films. His wife, the actress Yvonne Vallée, was his stage partner in French revues. "In private life, he is taciturn, aloof and more than a little cynical. His favorite diversion is roaming through the toughest districts of Paris, disguised as an apache; his greatest hatred is going to parties."

Sacha Guitry and Yvonne Printemps
November 1926, Paris
Walery
"The Guitrys, *M.* et *Mme.*, are the most popular comedians of the boulevards; . . . Guitry is a deft caricaturist as well as a keen satirist . . . after years as a farceur, he wrote in rapid succession a revue, a musical comedy, *L'Amour Masque,* and an operetta, *Mozart,* thereby making Mlle. Printemps a prima donna."

Ferenc Molnár and Lili Darvas
March 1928
Edward Steichen
"Through no rose-colored glass, but through his famous, flashing monocle, Molnár looks upon the world which is modern Hungary, and sees there the magic of drollery and despair going by in such gay carnival, such lilt of wit and wistfulness, as must make even a distant America grateful that *The Play's the Thing* and that Molnár is among the most prolific of modern playwrights."

Ruth Gordon
April 1929
Cecil Beaton
From her Broadway debut as Nibs in *Peter Pan* in 1915 to Hollywood stardom, Ruth Gordon acted in over fifty plays—four of which she herself had written. She is shown here in the title role of *Serena Blandish,* a satirical comedy by Enid Bagnold about the difficulty of getting married.

ylvia Sidney
August 1929
Edward Steichen
Still in her teens, Sidney had already gone to Hollywood and returned to Broadway. *V.F.* called her "A brittle comedienne and at the same time a wistful protagonist for tragedy."

H. L. Mencken
February 1927
Edward Steichen
"He is anti-Puritan, anti-democrat, anti-Christian and a Nietzschean individualist, 'America's Severest Critic.' He is an intellectual artistocrat, who, nonetheless, spends most of his time in describing and denouncing the average man. He disbelieves in practically everything American, especially in America's future, but is the eager champion of whatever is sound in American literature."

Sherwood Anderson
December 1926
Edward Steichen
Anderson had just written the novel *In Dark Laughter,* which Mencken characterized as having the cruel truthfulness of a snapshot. Mencken said of Anderson: "He seems to derive from no one, and to have no relation to any contemporary. An aloof, moody, often incoherent, mainly impenetrable man, he has made his own road."

Theodore Dreiser
June 1926
Charles Sheeler
"Dreiser lumbered out of the Midlands with *Sister Carrie* and with a peasant persistence championed the ordinary, commonplace man in fiction, with all his faults, vices and virtues, against the aristocratic tradition of 'nice people,' correct form and half truths."

François Mauriac
Unpublished, April 1929, Paris
Berenice Abbott
Mauriac achieved success in 1922 and 1923 with *Le Baiser au lépreux* and *Génitrix* (translations of both are in *The Family,* 1930). "He is a novelist who has been to Les Landes what Thomas Hardy was to Wessex."

Paul Valéry
October 1929
Aubes
Valéry was not yet twenty-one when he was recognized as a poet and essayist; however, he published very little until the age of forty-five in 1916. He succeeded Anatole France in the French Academy in 1925.

André Gide
January 1928, Paris
Berenice Abbott
Gide's novel of 1927, *The Counterfeiters,* had become a best seller in America. In 1928, in an essay *V.F.* entitled "Art and Artifice," he wrote: "Greece banished the man who added a string to the lyre. Art is born of constraint, lives on conflict, and dies of liberty."

Max Reinhardt
January 1928
Alexander Bengsch
The innovative and influential German theatrical producer and director staged gigantic productions, full of pageantry and color, and was especially noted for his direction of mob scenes. In 1920 he founded the Salzburg Festival; in 1928 *V.F.* called him "the world's best-known stage director."

Thomas Mann
May 1929
Photographer unidentified
Mann, the Nobel Laureate for Literature of 1929, was then living quietly in a suburb of Munich. "The clue to the temper of Thomas Mann, who is considered by many the greatest living writer of the Western World, is that he considers himself not an artist but as a good bourgeois who chanced to fall into the writing profession."

Walter Gropius
December 1928
Lucia Moholy-Dessau
Gropius, founder of the Bauhaus, at forty-five, on a visit to the United States. The trip strengthened his belief in the modernism movement.

Frederick Kiesler
May 1929
Photographer unidentified
An architect who devoted his attention to problems of the motion picture theater. He developed the funnel-shaped theater which provided improved vision for audiences.

Alma Gluck
January 1923, New York
Nickolas Muray
Opera star Alma Gluck, born in Romania, made her Metropolitan Opera debut in 1909, and by 1915 her royalties from phonograph records had exceeded those of any other artist, with the possible exception of Caruso. She was married to the renowned violinist Efrem Zimbalist, and her salon had become a center of musical and artistic life in New York.

Arturo Toscanini
March 1929, Parma
Vaghi
Toscanini was known always to conduct from memory (although sometimes with blank paper before him so as not to call the audience's attention to the feat). When told by actress Geraldine Farrar, who had just watched him conduct a rehearsal of the Metropolitan Opera orchestra, that he was the star of the performance, he was said to have replied: "Madame, there are no stars in performances. There are stars only in heaven."

Michael Arlen
December 1925
Gallo
The vogue of the Arlen books, *The Green Hat or Romance for a Few* and *These Charming People* made the opening of the stage version of *The Green Hat,* with Katharine Cornell and Leslie Howard, the most outstanding event of the theatrical season of 1925–1926. Alexander Woollcott wrote in 1925, "*The Green Hat* is the work of a young man who has said of himself 'I am only half-heartedly a realist and may yet live to be accused of shuffling humanity behind a phrase.' "

The Sitwells (Edith, Osbert, Sacheverell)
August 1929, London
Cecil Beaton
"The Sitwells, three porcelain exquisites, proceeding in unison with an almost persuasive concentration from one to another baroque posture, like the syllables in a charade that make no sense separately but may gather some meaning when assembled: Sacheverell, the name of a pre-Raphaelite ('mainly self-educated'); Osbert, the figure in profile at the lower right ('recreation: regretting the Bourbons'); and Edith, might be anything ('intense dislike for simplicity and a sense of humor')."

Cecil B. de Mille
Unpublished, no date
Edward Steichen
Jim Tully, in 1926, called de Mille "A Napoleon of Shadows. . . . He spent one hundred thousand dollars in getting the trick effect of the dividing of the Red Sea in *The Ten Commandments*. It was one of the most astonishing things ever done with the camera. . . . In fifty-six pictures, he has made fifty-four financial successes. He says frankly that he considers the two failures the most artistic."

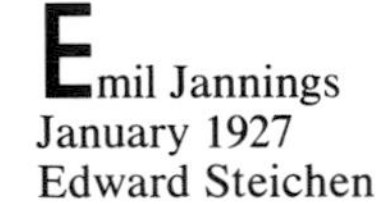
Emil Jannings
January 1927
Edward Steichen
This most famous of German screen actors of his time had recently arrived in the United States to make films in Hollywood. In November 1927, Jim Tully described some conversation with Jannings: " 'All my stories now have unhappy endings,' boomed the giant German through a giant interpreter. Over his moon-like face passed a cloud. He raised his powerful hand. 'I do not insist on the unhappy ending if it be not logical—in keeping,' he waved the hand—'with the story.' "

John Gilbert
May 1928
Edward Steichen
Gilbert was Garbo's dashing lover in *Flesh and the Devil* and other of her early pictures, and for a time her off-screen suitor. Said Jim Tully: "According to the M-G-M publicity writer, Mr. Gilbert's hobby is 'to be at ease.' His ambition is 'to be good.' His pastime is 'keeping in a good mood.' He 'hopes sometime to be a director.' "

Greta Garbo
October 1929
Edward Steichen
In 1934, Maddy Vectel characterized the typical romantic role played by Garbo: "Incapable of flirtations, and with a face and body too individual for fashionable 'chic,' she was, notwithstanding, put into fashionable clothes and told to portray international neurotics." At the time of this photograph, at twenty-four, Garbo was about to undertake a different sort of part, that of the cynical dockside ex-prostitute in the film adaptation of Eugene O'Neill's *Anna Christie*.

G. W. Pabst
July 1932
George Hoyningen-Huené
December 1932
George Hoyningen-Huené
He directed the famous *West Front* of 1918; Greta Garbo in her first picture, *Street of Sorrow,* in 1925; and *Atlantide.* "He sees the cinema as a social force."

Louise Brooks
January 1929, Los Angeles
Edward Steichen
"Long before her sultry Cleopatra bangs had created the head-dress known as 'a Louise Brooks,' this diminutive actress was touring the hinterlands as a young, callow dancer of the Denishawn troupe. After that her progress was swift, George White's *Scandals,* the Café de Paris of London, the *Ziegfeld Follies* as featured dancer. With her first heavy-lidded glances from the reels of Adolphe Menjou's *A Social Celebrity,* Miss Brooks made her debut as a Lorelei of the cinema." Brooks became the favored star of the Süd Film Company of Berlin, under the direction of G. W. Pabst, in films such as *Pandora's Box.*

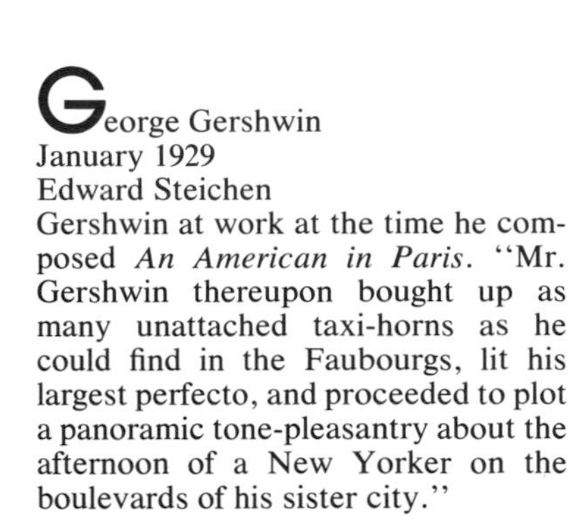

George Gershwin
January 1929
Edward Steichen
Gershwin at work at the time he composed *An American in Paris*. "Mr. Gershwin thereupon bought up as many unattached taxi-horns as he could find in the Faubourgs, lit his largest perfecto, and proceeded to plot a panoramic tone-pleasantry about the afternoon of a New Yorker on the boulevards of his sister city."

the
1930s

HAMILTON STANDARD
PROPELLER CORPORATION

Amelia Earhart
May 1932
Acme Newspictures
Earlier that year Earhart had become the first woman pilot to fly across the Atlantic alone. She had married the well-known publisher G. P. Putnam the year before.

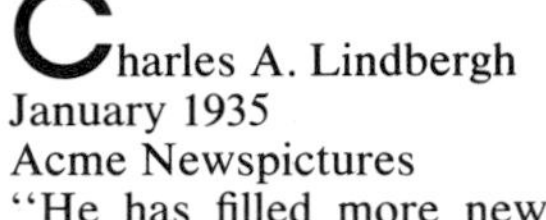

Charles A. Lindbergh
January 1935
Acme Newspictures
"He has filled more newspaper space then any living soul. He is one of our favorite heroes, and any newspaper that tried to put him in an unfavorable light would pass quietly out of existence."

Irving Thalberg and Norma Shearer
March 1932, Culver City
Edward Steichen

The blissful pair pictured here are the Canadian-born actress Norma Shearer and her husband, the legendary Irving Thalberg, then head of production for M-G-M. Shearer came to New York in 1920, and eventually to Hollywood, where she met Thalberg. The story is that at first his youthful appearance led her to think he was an office boy, a faux pas she finally lived down by marrying him three years later.

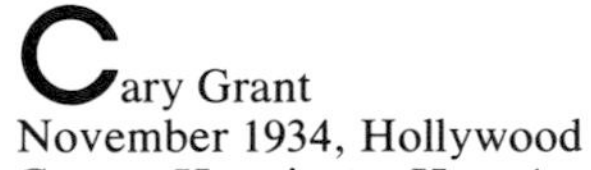

Cary Grant
November 1934, Hollywood
George Hoyningen-Huené

"It was not until Mae West looked at him from under her eyelids, and murmured throatily . . . warm, dark and handsome . . . and sighed, that Cary Grant really began to reap his just rewards from the public." This was in *She Done Him Wrong* in 1933, and from then until his retirement in 1969 the British actor was one of the most sought-after leading men in films.

Joan Blondell
May 1933, Hollywood
Imogen Cunningham
"Miss Blondell was born in New York and made her stage debut at the age of four months. She has played repertory in tank towns in China, one-night stands in Germany and split weeks in Australia. Two years ago she was on Broadway in *Penny Arcade,* with a young actor named James Cagney. Warner Brothers transplanted both the play and the players to Hollywood, where the team of Cagney and Blondell made cinema history last year in *Blonde Crazy* and *The Crowd Roars*."

James Cagney
September 1932, Hollywood
Imogen Cunningham
"Born on July 17, 1904, in a flat over his father's saloon on Eighth Street and Avenue D (the old Gashouse district), Cagney's career includes the following jobs: office boy on the New York *Sun,* bundle-wrapper at Wanamaker's, bellhop at the Friars Club, custodian of a New York Public Library branch, Columbia University student, artist, chorus boy, stage actor. His politics are radical; his hobby is boxing; his goal, Medicine."

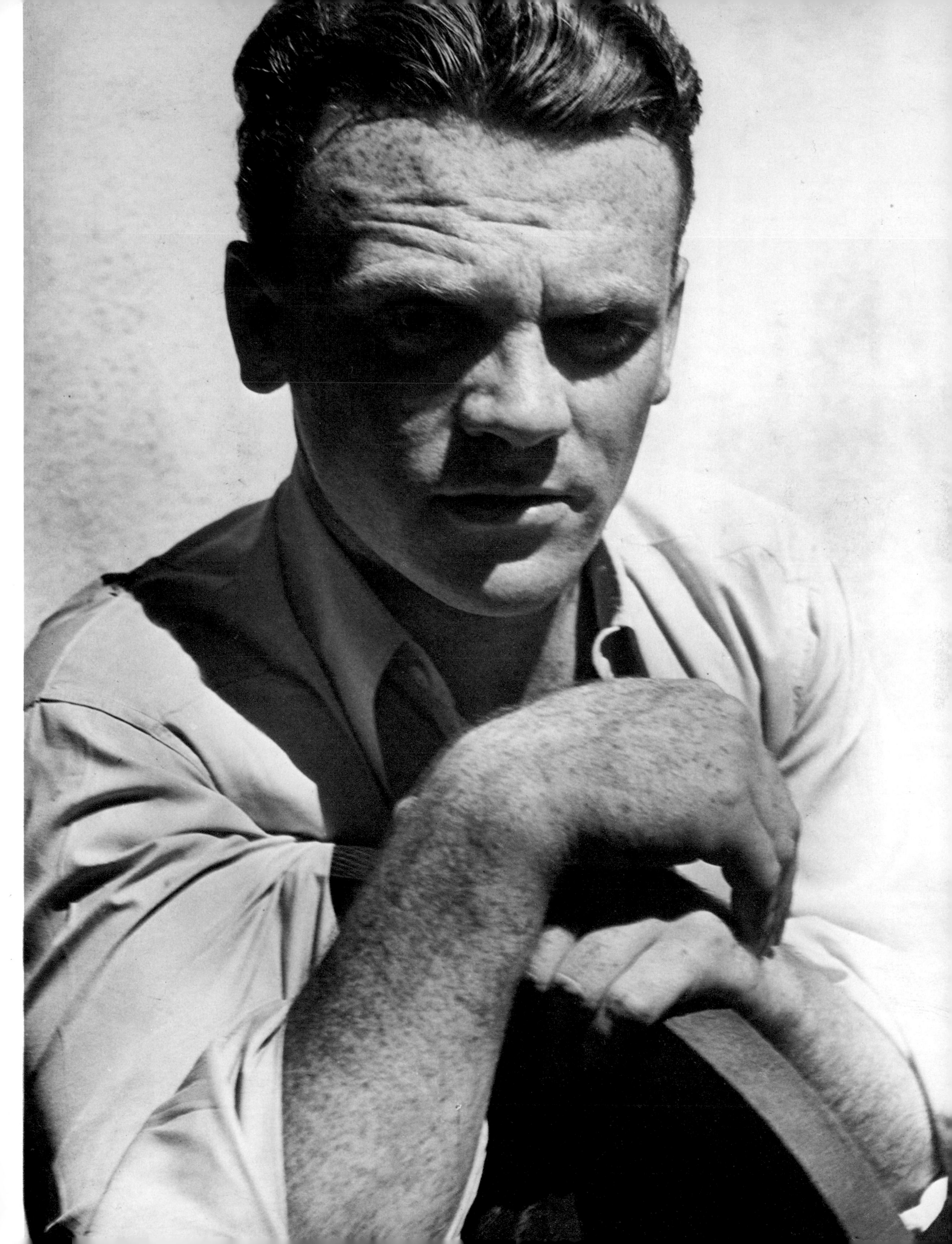

Jean Harlow
January 1935
George Hurrell
Harlow at twenty-four, two years before her death. "Born Harlean Carpenter in 1911 in Kansas City, Missouri, she eloped at 16, was divorced at 20. Her subsequent marriages and rumored romances have made newspaper history. Her next film will be *Spoiled;* she is the author of an unpublished novel, *Tonight is Today;* and she holds the unofficial dice record at Agua Caliente casino, with 34 straight passes."

Charles Spencer Chaplin
May 1931
Edward Steichen
According to Chaplin in *V.F.* one of his descriptions of his ideal woman was: "She knows the words of no popular dance music or, if she does, never sings them in my ear when dancing."/Pages 136–137.

Tallulah Bankhead
April 1931
Cecil Beaton
It was on the London stage that the Alabamian became famous. "She became, almost instantly, the giddiest kind of public idol. Her gowns, her gestures, her newest plays, her house in Mayfair have, for five years, been matters of passionate interest to that curiously eager and plaintive body, the British queue." She had recently returned to America to make her first film, *The Tarnished Lady*.

W. Somerset Maugham
May 1933
Cecil Beaton
"Following his first novel, *Liza of Lambeth,* in 1897, he wrote for 18 years before he finally tasted triumph, with *Of Human Bondage,* that epic of bitter wisdom, received at first with critical apathy, now considered one of the greatest books of the 20th century."

Dorothy Parker
May 1932
Edward Steichen
"Mrs. Parker is famous for three things: her dachshund, Robinson; her promptly columnized quips; and her quasi-cynical, quasi-sentimental, and impishly filliped verse, which has created a new genre among the younger and lighter poetasters of our speakeasy generation."

Colette
August 1935, New York
Edward Steichen
Gabrielle Sidonie Colette, shown here in her sixties, was the first woman in France to bob her hair—around the turn of the century. Widely considered France's foremost woman writer, she was the only woman elected to the Goncourt Academy during her lifetime.

James Joyce
January 1930, Paris
Berenice Abbott
Joyce at forty-eight was at work on *Finnegan's Wake,* then called *Work in Progress,* which *V.F.* described as revealing "that Mr. Joyce has swung off the edge of the earth, away from the gravitational force of all known traditions of language, and is writing in a puzzling idiom." Four more years were to pass before Federal judge John M. Woolsey—calling the book both "brilliant and dull," and stating that "while its effect is undoubtedly somewhat emetic, nowhere does it tend to be an aphrodisiac"—would make *Ulysses* legal in the United States.

Luigi Pirandello
October 1935
Edward Steichen
Pirandello, after receiving the 1934 Nobel Prize for Literature, at seventy-two, during his second visit to the United States. "He is now making plans to go to Hollywood for a first venture at the films . . . and his new book will bear the rebel-sounding title, *Information Concerning My Involuntary Sojourn on the Earth.*" He died a year later.

Six actors in search of an author
Unpublished, no date, Berlin
Zander and Labisch
The Berlin cast of Pirandello's play.

Constantin Brancusi
March 1934, Paris
Pierre Matisse
The Romanian sculptor, shown here at fifty-eight, went to live in Paris in 1904. Declining Rodin's invitation to work with him, Brancusi sculpted on his own, seldom emerging from his studio. About 1910 he began to develop marble and metal abstract pieces of two types: variations of the "egg" shape and "bird" motifs.

Diego Rivera
June 1933
Lusha Nelson
The Mexican Indian painter photographed while in the process of working on a prodigious mural for Rockefeller Center that caused a "momentous sensation." It was later rejected because it included a portrait of Lenin. The mural was close to being completed when it was destroyed.

José Clemente Orozco
June 1933
Edward Weston
This Mexican muralist (who had also been a successful architect and mathematician) was painting a set of frescoes in the Dartmouth College Library. The project was the largest of its kind ever undertaken in this country—three thousand square feet given to *The Epic of Culture in the New World*. It was one of three series of frescoes he executed in the United States from 1927 through 1932.

Serge Lifar
Unpublished, no date
George Hoyningen-Huené
Lifar, Russian dancer, choreographer, director, teacher, and dance historian, primarily self-taught, became Diaghilev's *premier danseur* in 1925. In 1933 *V.F.* noted, "Serge Lifar, the loudly trumpeted young aesthete who was Diaghilev's star pupil, makes his American debut this month."

Martha Graham
Unpublished, 1931
Edward Steichen
V.F., December 1931: "The rare phenomenon of an American audience cheering a native interpretive dancer occurred in New York last season at the conclusion of Martha Graham's compelling *Primitive Mysteries,* a composition which has been called the most significant piece of choreography yet to come out of America."

Salvador Dali
May 1930
Photographer unidentified
The young Spanish painter who lived in Paris "has had two one-man shows at the Julien Levy Galleries in New York within the past year (1934). His fantastic Surréaliste canvases have made him the most excitedly discussed contemporary painter."

Marcel Duchamp
July 1934
Lusha Nelson
Of Duchamp's most famous single work, *V.F.* had said in 1923: "*The Nude Descending the Staircase* and Duchamp walked up to fame. A sensation ten years ago, now an oracle." And in 1934: "that painting still draws puzzled crowds at Chicago's fair." Still an artist, Duchamp had become a ranking professional chess player.

Paul Klee
May 1930
Hugo Erfurth
Tristan Tzara wrote in 1923, "The painter who is the most remarkable personality of this school at Weimar is Paul Klee. . . . Musical assonances characterize his art-harmonic or capricious passages, the sound of discreet colors and the delicacy of forms. Klee has succeeded in creating an important work in a small compass, when all the other painters were working for an external monumentality. . . . It is by the freshness of its imagination and its grotesque and ironic spirit that his talent charms us."

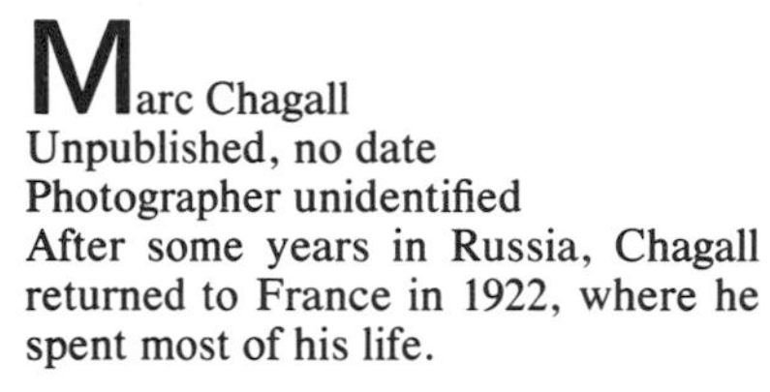

Marc Chagall
Unpublished, no date
Photographer unidentified
After some years in Russia, Chagall returned to France in 1922, where he spent most of his life.

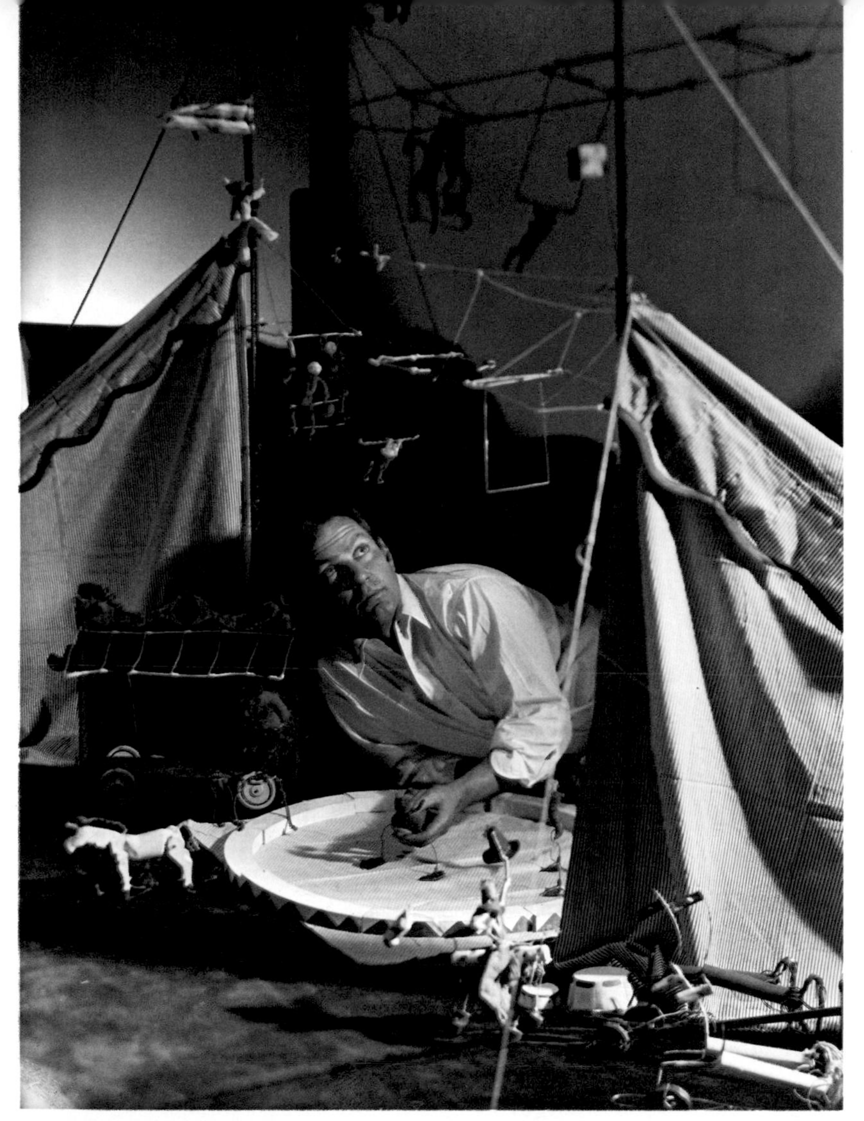

Alexander Calder
Unpublished, 1930
George Hoyningen-Huené
The inventor of the mobile, Calder had studied mechanical engineering. He had arrived in Paris in 1930, at the age of thirty-two, and was photographed with his toy circus construction.

Fernand Léger
Unpublished, 1929, Berlin
Riess
After World War I, Léger developed his characteristic style inspired by machine and industrial motifs. He created the first animated film, *Le Ballet mécanique,* in 1924: "I only utilize the visual values of the moment," he said. "We live in an epoch of contrasts and I wish to live at the height of my epoch."

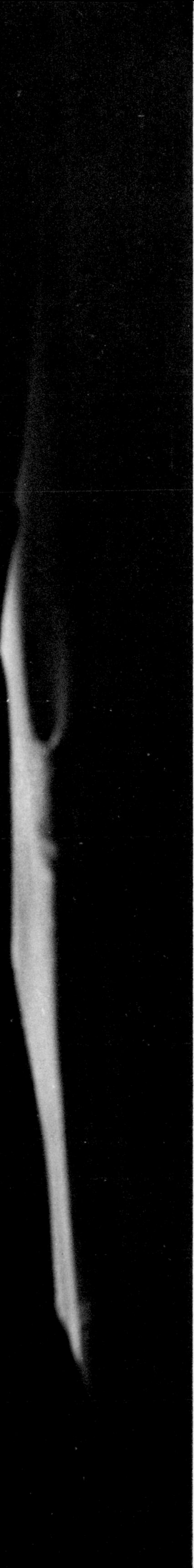

Laurence Kerr Olivier
Unpublished, no date
Cecil Beaton
Olivier made his stage debut at Stratford-on-Avon in 1922 at fifteen and achieved renown through his work with the Old Vic Company. In the thirties he was already known for his versatility: classics, modern plays, and comedy.

Noel Coward
November 1932
Edward Steichen
Coward at thirty-three, shortly before the opening of his *Design for Living,* starring Lynn Fontanne, Alfred Lunt, and himself. "His present mastery of the theater began when, as a pernicious choir boy of ten, he went on the stage as a child-actor and stayed on it long enough to undertake in 1913 the role of Slightly Soiled in *Peter Pan.*"

Tilly Losch
Unpublished, 1934
Cecil Beaton
Tilly Losch, a favored Viennese beauty, was a dancer, choreographer, and set designer. She appeared in many scenes of her own design.

Cole Porter
Unpublished, 1934
Horst
V.F. wrote, "His music expresses better than any other the bright spirit of the 1930s." Composer and lyricist he had already written "Let's Misbehave," and "What Is This Thing Called Love?" "He is the possessor," wrote Charles Shaw, "of a Croix de Guerre and belongs to the Racquet and Tennis Club of New York and the Traveler's of Paris. His favorite music is that of Stravinsky, Bach, Gershwin, and Rodgers; his favorite lyric writer, P. G. Wodehouse. He almost never goes to concerts."

Beatrice Lillie and Hope Williams
April 1932
Von Horn
These two were starring in Bernard Shaw's new play, *Too True to Be Good.* Cecil Beaton wrote: "Beatrice Lillie holds up to ridicule all those ladies who attempt to be just a bit more elegant than they can successfully be, and she has perhaps had a wider influence (what with all the debutantes and dowagers who have been going about in that refined falsetto accompanied by a swinging salute of the forefinger) than any comedienne of her day."

Bill (Bojangles) Robinson
June 1935, Hollywood
George Hurrell
The world's number one tap dancer at age fifty-eight. "Although he has been a professional entertainer for half a century . . . Bill Robinson—known to Harlem as 'Bojangles'—only recently made his cinema debut, in support of Miss Shirley Temple in *The Little Colonel*."

Louis Armstrong
November 1935
Anton Bruehl
"Jazz dazzler—maddest monarch of hot music is startling Gotham this season. . . . He played before the king of England, at His Majesty's express command, and the Palladium Theatre in London gave him the trumpet on which he now performs—gold-plated with ivory-tipped keys."

Carl Sandburg
April 1934
Edward Steichen
Poet, biographer of Abraham Lincoln, and writer of stories for children, Sandburg had also been a journalist. In 1922 *V.F.* said that his pamphlet on the Chicago race riots was "the most vivid and accurate account of them." Sandburg was Steichen's brother-in-law.

Paul Robeson
August 1933
Edward Steichen
Robeson as Brutus Jones, the Pullman porter who became a king, in the screen version of Eugene O'Neill's *The Emperor Jones*. A Phi Beta Kappa graduate of the Columbia University law school, singer of distinction, scholar, indomitable athlete, he began his acting career with the Provincetown Players in 1924. O'Neill chose the unknown Robeson to star in his new play *All God's Chillun Got Wings*, as well as a revival of *The Emperor Jones*.

Franklin Delano Roosevelt
and family
December 1932
Keystone View Company, Bachrach
The young lawyer and his family in 1916.

Franklin Delano Roosevelt
December 1932
Harris and Ewing
As Democratic nominee for vice-president in 1920, years before he was stricken with polio.

Neville Chamberlain
April 1933
Culver Pictures
"Chamberlain holds his umbrella up against the high winds of inflation."

Winston Churchill
April 1932 (variation)
Edward Steichen
In 1931 Harold Nicolson said of Winston Churchill in *V.F.,* "He was a Member of Parliament before he was twenty-seven, a Member of the Ministry before he was thirty-one, and a full-blown Cabinet Minister at thirty-four. . . . He is a man who leads forlorn hopes, and when the hopes of England become forlorn, he will once again be summoned to leadership."

Sigmund Freud
April 1932
Culver Pictures
Julian Huxley wrote in 1937: "Many disagree with Freud, disliking the emphasis he lays on man's 'baser nature,' others differ on intellectual or scientific grounds. But even if all the details of his system were wrong (which they are not) the fact remains that the oft-derided dream-doctor is one of the greatest living scientists, and the most notable explorer of new continents of the mind."

Otto Spengler
Unpublished, no date
James Abbé
The German philosopher and historian in Munich. In 1932, *V.F.* said of his latest work, *Man and Technics:* "Just as Spengler surveyed our Western civilization [in *Decline of the West*] and traced the curve of its inevitable and natural dissolution, so he now describes the equally inevitable triumph of the machine and the revolt against machinery of the superior man."

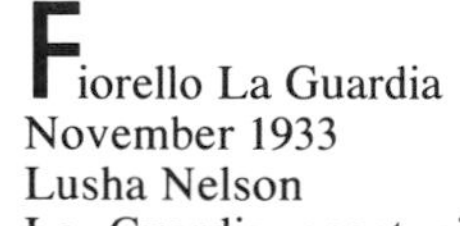
Fiorello La Guardia
November 1933
Lusha Nelson
La Guardia spent sixteen years in Congress, where he was a colorful and dynamic figure, but it was not until he was elected Mayor of New York City on the Fusion ticket in 1933 that his liberal views and fighting spirit aroused international interest.

Robert Moses
July 1935
Edward Steichen
Moses had served his first year and a half as New York City Parks Commissioner, an office he would hold until 1960. The Republican candidate for governor of New York in 1934, he took the worst beating theretofore on record. "The politicians don't like him, and they control the votes," observed Milton Mackaye in *V.F.*

Walter Lippmann
May 1933
Edward Steichen
From the 1920s to the 1960s Lippmann's counsel was sought and often heeded on monumental matters by every president from Woodrow Wilson to Lyndon Johnson. In an essay in 1928, Lippmann wrote: "The notion that the righteous minority can legislate the majority up to its own standards is, I think, a primary illusion of politically inexperienced people."

Clare Boothe Brokaw
August 1934
Cecil Beaton
Here she is before becoming Mrs. Henry Luce, before *The Women*, before becoming a congresswoman and an ambassador and a war correspondent. But already she had written a play *(Naomi's Daughter)* and a book *(Stuffed Shirts)* and a newspaper column, and had been managing editor of *V.F.*, where her colleagues noted that she combined "a fragile blondeness with a will of steel."

Jack Dempsey
March 1932
Edward Steichen
In 1926, Dempsey had lost the World Heavyweight Championship to Gene Tunney. At the time of this photograph, Paul Gallico wrote: "For many months Colorado Jack has been searching the answer to the question that every pugilist asks himself at one time or other: Am I good enough to come back?"

Primo Carnera
June 1934
Edward Steichen
Carnera, on the eve of his fight with Max Baer for the heavyweight championship of the world. Gallico wrote: "Primo is very sensitive about the size of his feet and may be kidded into bridling and blushing at which time he may be struck a violent blow on almost any part of his anatomy." Baer won.

Joe Louis
October 1935
Lusha Nelson
"On the summer night of June 25, [1935] at the Yankee Stadium in New York, Mr. Louis will quarrel with Primo Carnera, the quondam champion, for fifteen rounds. . . . his record, since he began fighting for money a year ago, is almost without blemish —18 knockouts out of 22 starts." Louis won, and two years later became World Heavyweight Champion.

Jesse Owens
September 1935
Lusha Nelson
Paul Gallico predicted of Jesse Owens, "This remarkable one-man track team, along with Eulace Peacock, will probably win between them some five or six events for the United States in the forthcoming Olympic games in Berlin next summer." In fact at the 1936 Olympic games in Berlin, Jesse Owens astounded the world and upset Hitler's "Aryan" theories by equaling the world mark (10.3 seconds) in the 100-meter race and breaking world records in the 200-meter race (20.7 seconds) and the broad jump (26 feet 5⅜ inches). His records lasted for more than twenty years./Page 176.

Bill Tilden
July 1934
Acme Newspictures
The lanky figure of this king of the courts completely dominated American lawn tennis for many years. In 1924 *V.F.* called Tilden "the outstanding tennis figure in the world."/Page 177.

Arnold Schoenberg
April 1930, Paris
Man Ray
The Austrian composer seven years after he had developed the twelve-tone scale. In 1925, Virgil Thomson wrote, "Now the ultimate of chromaticism, of incessant modulation, is a completely flexible harmony which is never in any definite key at all. Such is the model, conscious or unconscious, for most contemporary writing in Germany, Austria and Hungary."

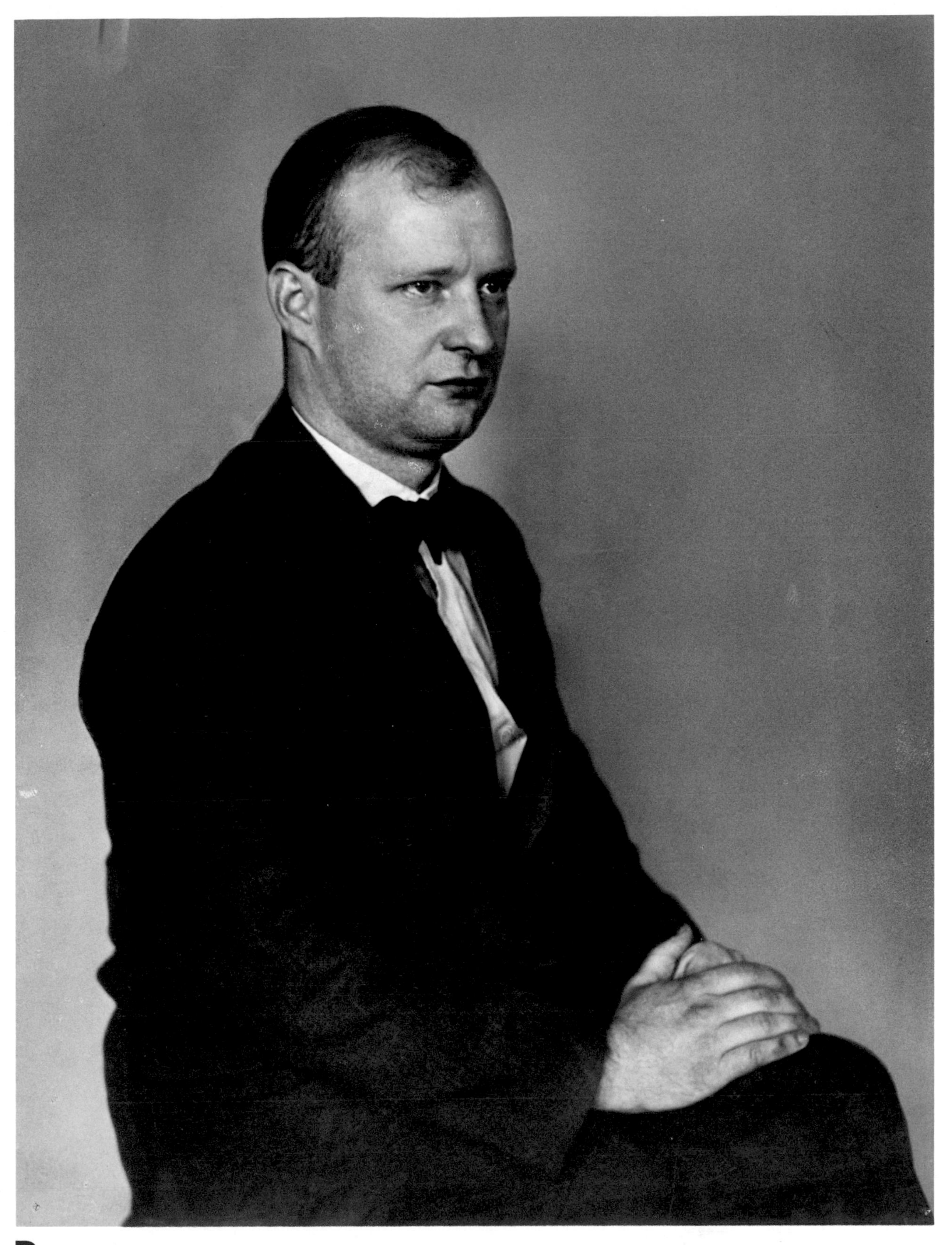

Paul Hindemith
August 1930
August Sander
At thirty-five Hindemith was already known as the leader of atonal music in Germany. His latest opera, *Cardillac,* had been a great success. Four years later the Nazi government banned public performance of his music.

Kurt Weill
Unpublished, 1933, Paris
George Hoyningen-Huené
Weill first became known for his short, satirical, surrealist operas. *Dreigroshenoper,* a modern version of John Gay's *Beggar's Opera,* with a book by Bertolt Brecht, translated by Marc Blitzstein was first produced as *The Threepenny Opera* in New York in 1933. His works were condemned by the Nazis, and, in 1933, Weill left Germany.

Ernst Lubitsch
December 1932, Hollywood
Imogen Cunningham
At age nineteen Lubitsch toured Europe for a season in Max Reinhardt's production of *Faust* and later appeared as dancer and grotesque in a number of Reinhardt's ballets. He first became known as a film director through *Passion* and *Gypsy Blood* in which he introduced Pola Negri. Jim Tully of *V.F.* asked: "Mr. Lubitsch, why is it you are satisfied to direct light comedy when you might do another *Passion?*" "Molière was content to do comedy," was his reply.

Elisabeth Bergner
April 1933
George Hoyningen-Huené
This prominent Viennese actress had her greatest successes in English plays, including *The Last of Mrs. Cheney* and *Saint Joan,* which was produced by Max Reinhardt. By 1934 she was in exile from Germany, where her film *Catherine the Great* was banned.

Gustav Gründgens
Unpublished, no date
George Hoyningen-Huené
He started his career at the prestigious theater in Hamburg, Germany, Hamburger Kammerspiel, where he played fashionable villians and dandies. His greatest role was as Mephisto in Goethe's *Faust,* which he performed over six hundred times. In 1934 he became a protégé of Goering, who made Gründgens the director of the German State Theater in Berlin. He became a Nazi but never a member of the party.

Josef Von Sternberg
March 1932
Edward Steichen
"His directorial genius burned away completely unnoticed save for one brief rocket flare, *The Salvation Hunters,* in 1924, until five years ago, when von Sternberg focused the attention of all the cinema sophisticates upon himself and his work by the technical adroitness which he brought to his filming of *Underworld,*" wrote *V.F.* He had recently discovered Marlene Dietrich, who appeared in his latest film, *Shanghai Express.*

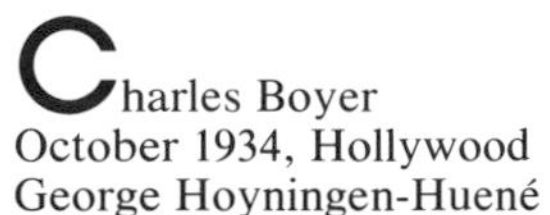

Charles Boyer
October 1934, Hollywood
George Hoyningen-Huené
Boyer had been in the theater since 1920 and was "a furore in France." However, his first efforts in American movies were less than successful; after a series of bit roles in the early '30s (he was Jean Harlow's chauffeur in *Red-Headed Woman*), he returned to Paris. In 1934 he was persuaded to return by Erik Charell, the German director, who starred him in *Caravan,* and launched his Hollywood career.

Marlene Dietrich
March 1934, Hollywood
Edward Steichen
"Mary Magdalene Dietrich, called Marlene (pronounced Marlain-ah), was born in Berlin and studied the violin until overpracticing injured her left hand, when she went on the stage in the German version of *Broadway,* the American success. Josef Von Sternberg, the Paramount director, saw her in Berlin and selected her to play in *The Blue Angel* with Emil Jannings, and in *Morocco,* with Gary Cooper."

Peter Lorre
January 1936
Lusha Nelson
Lorre at thirty-one, not long after his arrival in Hollywood. "Born in Hungary's Carpathian mountains, Lorre never entered a theater until he became an actor. . . . He ran away from home at seventeen, slept in public parks, nearly starved, worked briefly in a Viennese bank, finally got a walk-on part, with no lines, in a Breslau production of *Danton*." His film debut in Fritz Lang's *M,* in 1931, had brought him critical acclaim.

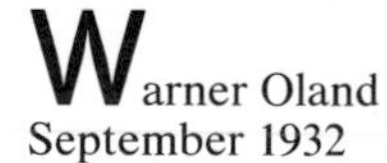

Warner Oland
September 1932
Imogen Cunningham
Warner Oland, a Swede by birth, was usually cast as an Oriental. He had been playing villains since the days of Theda Bara, but his best-known characterizations were Charlie Chan and Dr. Fu Manchu.

Bette Davis
February 1935
Maurice Goldberg
"Bette Davis is one of the Bright Young People of the cinema, a notable representative of an entirely new type of screen player which has developed in the past two years. It consists of young men and women who treat motion pictures as a serious profession and go about it with ambitious diligence, as opposed to the pretty moppets of the past who used to drift into the film after having been crowned Miss Oscawana of 1920 at the Elks Ball."

Leslie Howard
January 1934
Edward Steichen
Since World War I, the American stage had beckoned many of the best young English players, among them Leslie Howard. In 1927 *V.F.* described *Her Cardboard Lover,* in which he played opposite Jeanne Eagels: "Its first New York performance was marked by the distressing behavior of an audience so unruly that it kept yelling 'Howard, Howard' all the time Miss Eagels was taking her curtain calls."

Gary Cooper
February 1930, Los Angeles
Edward Steichen
"When Gary Cooper left Grinnel College in Iowa, he went to work as a cartoonist on a Helena newspaper," wrote *V.F.* in 1931; "but some stirring within (or maybe his drawings weren't so good) urged him to seek the legendary gold in the hills of the Golden State. Arriving in Los Angeles with two hundred dollars, he soon found that being a photographer's assistant was not profitable; so he fell in with the nearest crowd and found himself an extra in a movie studio."

Carole Lombard
July 1931, Hollywood
Cecil Beaton
"Here is another of those fabulous young women who graduated from Mack Sennett comedies—only a year or so ago, in this case—to leading roles on the screen. Miss Lombard recently changed her name—on the advice of an astrologer from Carol to Carole, and will play opposite Gary Cooper in *I Take This Woman,* a Western romance."

Preston Sturges
May 1930
Arnold Schröder
"Over the theatrical horizon last autumn came Preston Sturges, suave and unpretentious, with a new play, *Strictly Dishonorable*—a comedy so excellent, so impeccable in structure and dialogue that, on its opening night the bravos of audience and critics echoed lustily into the dawn."

Ginger Rogers
September 1930
Von Horn
"A new comedienne of the stage and screen, soon to play the leading feminine role opposite Bert Lahr in his new musical comedy, *Girl Crazy*. . . . Four years ago a fourteen-year-old girl with a future came out of Independence, Missouri, to win a Charleston contest in Dallas, Texas—with a prize of four weeks in vaudeville."

Jean Arthur
August 1935
Lusha Nelson
"Miss Arthur is that peculiar phenomenon, a native New Yorker; her earliest goal was the career of a tightrope walker; she was actually trained to teach French and German; but her first job was a commercial artist's model in New York."

William Powell
December 1930
Barnaba
"Like many other young men whose parents wish them to become lawyers, William Powell became an actor at an early age. . . . In a recent series of talking pictures . . . Powell established himself securely as an unsurpassed hero of those screen stories in which the action is suave and lightly accented by top hats, expensive cigarettes and perfect manners, and the dirty work delicately handled."

Katharine Hepburn
July 1934
Cecil Beaton
"Miss Hepburn, the stormy petrel of the RKO studios and a subject for raging controversy on two continents, will next appear in Sir James M. Barrie's *The Little Minister*—a role which should further deify her in the hearts of those admirers who still swoon at the memory of *Little Women*." Her first film, *A Bill of Divorcement*, had brought her instantaneous fame.

Spencer Tracy
December 1934, Hollywood
Imogen Cunningham
The thirty-four-year-old Tracy had just begun his film work in 1930. This photograph was taken on a back lot by the young art photographer Imogen Cunningham. Before the end of the decade he would win two Academy Awards, for *Captains Courageous* (1937) and *Boys Town* (1938).

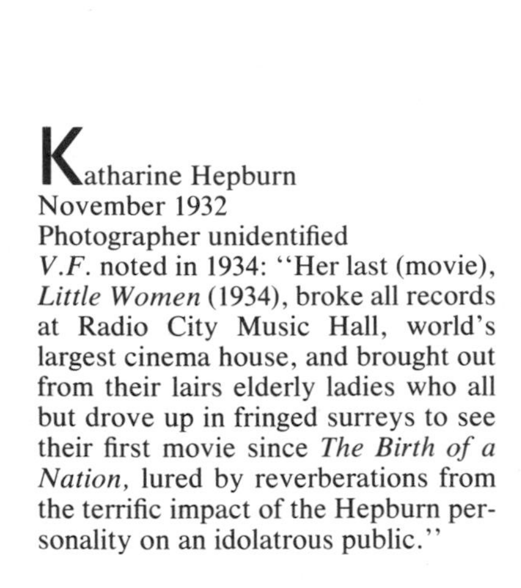

Katharine Hepburn
November 1932
Photographer unidentified
V.F. noted in 1934: ''Her last (movie), *Little Women* (1934), broke all records at Radio City Music Hall, world's largest cinema house, and brought out from their lairs elderly ladies who all but drove up in fringed surreys to see their first movie since *The Birth of a Nation,* lured by reverberations from the terrific impact of the Hepburn personality on an idolatrous public.''

Arnold Genthe
February 1923
Nickolas Muray

Baron de Meyer
Unpublished, 1932
George Hoyningen-Huené

THE PHOTOGRAPHERS

ARNOLD GENTHE 1869–1942

Born in Berlin, Genthe attended the universities of Berlin and Jena, where he received his doctorate in 1894. A highly qualified philologist, he had mastered eight ancient and modern languages before coming to San Francisco in 1895 as a tutor for some young German counts. He began his work in photography in 1896 on the highly acclaimed "Chinatown series" and opened a portrait studio in 1899. He worked there as a professional portrait photographer, and in addition to the portraits, he photographed the aftermath of the San Francisco earthquake and fire.

After arriving in New York in 1911 he continued portraiture, photographing many renowned people of the day: John Galsworthy, John Barrymore, Toscanini, Paderewski, Mary Pickford, Andrew Mellon, and President Woodrow Wilson. Genthe had no compunctions about retouching his negatives to obscure distracting detail, and enhanced his subjects dramatically by this means. His portraits first appeared in *Vanity Fair* in March 1915 and were used consistently until 1926.

Many of his studies are interesting as period pieces, but three of his most unforgettable images are his profiles of the famed Eleanora Duse; the young, virtually unknown Garbo; and one of his favorite subjects, the torso of Isadora Duncan in flight. All of these first appeared in *Vanity Fair*.

Crowninshield offered Genthe the job of staff photographer, later accepted by Steichen. Genthe turned it down because he refused to be edited by anyone, even Crowninshield.

MALCOLM ARBUTHNOT 1874–1968

Arbuthnot was an English portrait photographer, virtually unknown in this country. In 1914 he married a Kodak heiress and established his portrait studio at 43-44 New Bond Street, London. After the first World War he took many photographs for the *Illustrated London News*. Arbuthnot was considered primarily a commercial studio photographer who photographed actors, actresses, and some of the more noted personalities: Ezra Pound, George Bernard Shaw, Augustus John, Henri Matisse, Joseph Conrad, Irene Castle. His work had a controlled tonality and unusual tenderness of approach, as he sought to portray each individual's character. Later, all of his negatives were destroyed in a fire on New Bond Street, and discouraged by the great loss, he gave up his photographic work.

BARON GAYNE DE MEYER c. 1869–1946

Born De Meyer Watson, of a French father and a Scottish mother, de Meyer was brought up in Saxony. Moving to London he married a fascinating young woman who was said to be the daughter of either King Edward VII or Kaiser Wilhelm II. He and his wife entertained in an exotically

Edward Steichen
October 1929
Self-portrait

Nickolas Muray
December 1926
Edward Steichen

James Abbé
February 1934
Howard Coster

decorated London town house.

De Meyer's earliest photographs, emphasizing somber shadows and aesthetic subjects, were taken under the influence of Alfred Stieglitz. Then he invented a new world by using artificial light to make an aurora borealis effect, employing a soft-focus yet pinpoint-sharp lens to give an extra sparkle to shiny surfaces, and printing his photographs on delicate platinum paper to create dazzling whites and silvers. De Meyer was never interested in photographing "character," but rather poses suggesting elegance, fantasy, and spirit. His highly refined art suited the people who were his subjects.

The search for original photographic images led Condé Nast to Baron de Meyer, who at that time was not a professional photographer but a man of leisure who took his beautiful photographs solely for his own pleasure. Condé Nast was struck by their quality and persuaded the baron to take up photography as a business and to work exclusively for his publications. De Meyer became one of the stable of photographers for *Vogue* and *Vanity Fair* from 1914 to 1920.

EDWARD STEICHEN 1879–1973

Shortly after Frank Crowninshield published Steichen's self-portrait in *Vanity Fair* captioned "the world's best photographer," Steichen became a star photographer for both *Vogue* and *Vanity Fair.*

Born in Luxembourg, Steichen moved to Hancock, Michigan, in 1881 and on to Milwaukee in 1889 where the young Steichen began his studies in painting, which he intended to make his life work. His formal education ended at fifteen, when he began a four-year apprenticeship with a Milwaukee lithography company and used photographs as a basis for his poster designs. He photographed "details" of the countryside and sold his pictures for posters. The fashionable romanticism of the day led him to try to create "art" through the lens of the camera, resulting in dark, foggy pictures.

He met Alfred Stieglitz in 1902 and showed fourteen of his photographs in Stieglitz's exhibition American Photography. He helped found Photo-Secession (a group of photographers who asserted the expressive possibilities of photography and claimed it to be an independent art form), designed the cover of its quarterly, *Camera Work,* and helped establish and design the Photo-Secession Galleries at 291 Fifth Avenue. Steichen then went to Paris to concentrate on painting. There his friendship with Rodin gave him superlative photographic opportunities, and he produced an extraordinary series of pigment prints of Rodin and his sculpture.

Back in New York, still under the strong influence of Stieglitz, Steichen took impressionistic pictures of the Brooklyn Bridge and the Flatiron Building. His portraits at that time were often heavily "doctored": his self-portrait, for example, is so reworked that it might have been mistaken for an etching or a lithograph.

After the sinking of the *Lusitania,* Steichen immediately joined the photographic section of the Signal Corps. When World War I was over he experimented with photographic techniques. He took the most elaborate measures to photo-

Man Ray
November 1922
Self-portrait

Berenice Abbott
Unpublished, 1922, Paris
Man Ray

Cecil Beaton
Unpublished, no date
Self-portrait

graph objects in great detail, attempting to capture their exact value, scale, and weight. Having long since taken off his soft-focus lens, Steichen concentrated on photographing foxgloves and household utensils in needle-sharp close-ups. He made a thousand negatives of such objects as an apple and a white cup and saucer.

Steichen enlivened the idea of what a portrait could be in an era when most photography was stiff and inhuman. The portraits of Garbo and J. Pierpont Morgan show a tremendous vitality and strength. He consistently broke with tradition in portraiture, pioneering new ways of seeing a character before the lens and fixing in our minds forever such faces as Paul Robeson, Gloria Swanson, and George Gershwin. Steichen had the extraordinary ability to make his subjects come alive.

NICKOLAS MURAY 1892–1965

Born in Szeged, Hungary, Muray studied lithography, photoengraving, and the fundamentals of photography in Budapest. He came to the United States as an engraver in the European craftsman tradition with twenty-five dollars and a fifty-word English vocabulary. Immediately upon his arrival he was employed by Condé Nast as a photoengraver, doing color separations and halftone negatives.

In 1920 Muray opened a portrait studio on MacDougal Street and continued to support himself as a union engraver. At the same time his celebrity portraits began appearing in *Vanity Fair*. By 1925 he had established himself as a commercial portrait photographer and moved his studio to East Fiftieth Street. He was sent on assignment by *Vanity Fair* in 1926 to London, Paris, and Berlin to photograph the great and famous, among whom were George Bernard Shaw, H. G. Wells, John Galsworthy, and Claude Monet. His largest single assignment from *Vanity Fair* came in 1920 when he was hired to photograph movie stars in Hollywood —Douglas Fairbanks, Sr., and his wife, Mary Pickford, and his son and daughter-in-law, Joan Crawford. His fame rests on his celebrity portraits of Clarence Darrow and Calvin Coolidge, both seen in direct frontal poses in contrast to portraits of women, such as Alma Gluck and Elinor Wylie, who were often captured in more stylized poses.

JAMES ABBÉ 1883–1973

James Abbé was born in Alfred, Maine. While still a boy, he moved with his family to Newport News, Virginia, where he photographed ships and sailors and sold Kodak cameras in his father's bookstore. Abbé's pictures of the early film stars were valuable because they showed the well-known stars in a more intimate manner than did the routine studio portraits. Throughout the 1920s he used the cumbersome view-camera. Abbé later said, "Because of the necessary time exposures, I'd frequently resort to the Mathew Brady technique of virtually hypnotizing my subject while I exposed the film."

In the 1930s while working in France and Germany, Abbé went on to combine writing with photography and became a pioneer in photojournalism. From there it was a natural step to war correspondent. After the war, he became a radio news commentator and television critic in San Francisco. However, Abbé is best known for his portraits made in the twenties, which are most memorable. Abbé said of photography, "My early feeling about the power of the camera was that it was my own Aladin's lamp . . . like having a personal genie that could take me anywhere."

MAN RAY 1890–1976

Man Ray was born in Philadelphia as Emmanuel Rudnitsky. From 1908 to 1912, he studied architectural drawing and engineering at the Academy of Fine Arts and the Ferrer School in New York. His first jobs were in layout, lettering, typography, and graphic design, though he continued to draw and paint in his spare time. In 1910 he met Alfred Stieglitz at his gallery "291" and became a frequent visitor. He exhibited his paintings in 1915 at Charles Daniels's avant-garde gallery in New York, met Marcel Duchamp, and began making collages and assemblages.

In 1918 he bought a camera to make photographs of his paintings and soon after began experimenting with the range of creative possibilities photography offered him.

Man Ray moved to Paris in 1921 and worked as a professional fashion and portrait photographer. His portraits of Gertrude Stein, Tristan Tzara, Bronislava Nijinska, and Arnold Schoenberg demonstrate a unique point of view, possibly because his sitters were also his close friends.

BERENICE ABBOTT 1898–

Born in Springfield, Ohio, Abbott studied sculpture in New York, Berlin, and Paris with Bourdelle and Brancusi. She became Man Ray's assistant in 1923 and learned photographic technique and processing from him. In 1925 Abbott established her own photographic studio, which became a gathering place for the Parisian intelligentsia. Her portraits immortalized such greats as James Joyce, André Gide, Jean Cocteau, Marcel Duchamp, Djuna Barnes, and Peggy Guggenheim.

She returned to New York in 1929 and supported herself with free-lance portraiture and photojournalism for such magazines as *Fortune* and *Life*. She is best known for the work done on a federal art project grant from 1935 to 1939, entitled *Changing New York*. For this project she thoroughly documented New York as Atget had earlier documented Paris.

IMOGEN CUNNINGHAM 1883–1976

Born in Portland, Oregon, Cunningham at the age of eight saw photographs by Gertrude Käsebier reproduced in *The Craftsman* magazine and became interested in photography. She bought her first camera and soon after, took a correspondence course, and from 1903 until 1907 studied chemistry at the University of Washington. After graduation she took a job at the studio of Edward S. Curtis in Seattle, Washington, and printed hundreds of Curtis's negatives of Indians onto platinum paper. She was awarded a national scholarship to study photographic chemistry at the Technische Hochschule in Dresden.

En route from Germany to Seattle in 1910, she met Alfred Stieglitz and Gertrude Käsebier in New York. She opened a portrait studio in Seattle and continued photographing in a soft-focus style. In 1923 she met photographer Edward Weston, and her style changed significantly, assuming a new realism: her subjects came into sharp focus and her forms became clean and simple. She made closeup studies of flowers, which were exhibited at the Deutsche Werkbund exhibition Film and Foto, Stuttgart, 1929.

In 1930 she began to make many portraits of artists, writers, and photographers, and also started a series on movie stars for *Vanity Fair,* some of which appear here. Her closeup naturalistic studies of the young James Cagney and Joan Blondell convey a haunting magnetic quality.

CECIL BEATON 1904–1980

Born in London, Beaton turned to photography while still a child, photographing on vacations and collecting postcards and photographs. At twelve he used a wine cooler for a tripod. Later, on vacations from Harrow and Cambridge, he transformed his parents' bathroom into a makeshift darkroom, and at twenty saw his photographs published in *Vogue*.

In 1926 he went to Venice where he met Serge Diaghilev, impresario of the Ballet Russe, who encouraged him in photography. Upon his return to London, he opened a portrait studio in his father's house. With his increasing success as a portraitist, he became known for his "modernistic" style. He became staff photographer for both *Vogue* and *Vanity Fair,* and his pictures of cinema stars and actresses were popular for their general air of whimsy. Always open to experimentation, he would stop at nothing to create an image—as his photographs testify—filling the frame with double or triple exposures or props of all sorts and even going outdoors. Photography was just one aspect of Beaton's work; his other accomplishments as author, set and costume designer, and painter made him an important figure in the art and theater world.

INDEX

Page numbers in *italics* refer to illustrations